# NO

# PRISSY

# SHOES

Lord, uphold our steps in Your paths!

Ps. 17:5

Linda

# NO PRISSY SHOES

*Trusting God to Walk You Through Your Breast Cancer Journey*

## LINDA GRABEMAN

Pleasant Word
A Division of WinePress Group

Author's headshot taken by Laura Hutto, Shades of Gray photography—laurahutto.com

Pleasant Word (a division of WinePress Publishing, PO Box 428, Enumclaw, WA 98022) functions only as book publisher. As such, the ultimate design, content, editorial accuracy, and views expressed or implied in this work are those of the author.

ISBN 13: 978-1-4141-1670-9
ISBN 10: 1-4141-1670-5
Library of Congress Catalog Card Number: 2009914232

God has truly been the inspiration, composer, compiler, and editor of *No Prissy Shoes*. Any mistakes in this text are not in His speaking, but in my hearing. Therefore, I humbly dedicate this work to its Maker.

"God can do anything, you know—far more than you could ever imagine or guess or request in your wildest dreams! He does it not by pushing us around but by working within us, His Spirit deeply and gently within us."

—Ephesians 3:20

# CONTENTS

# ACKNOWLEDGMENTS

*T*HIS BOOK, AND my entire life, is one very large thank you note: To my precious husband, Dave, who "bears all things, believes all things, hopes all things, and endures all things." Thank you for encouraging and enabling me to follow God's leading in my life. I love you so.

To my wonderful sons, Christian and Carey: Thanks for being so tender and attentive to me when I was fragile. What a gift God has given me in watching you become men. Always live for Jesus. He has perfect plans for both of you, and I can't wait to see them unfold.

To my darling daughter, Chloe: You are wise beyond your years. It is a joy to watch you grow into your prophetic calling. Your deep love of the Word fills my heart with praise.

To my spiritual family at All Saints Church, the prayer chain, prayer teams, clergy and laity: For the past twenty-five years, you have loved, upheld, nurtured, and fed me. My love for you as the body of Christ will last throughout eternity.

To Bishop Alex Dickson, my spiritual mentor throughout this journey: You have "the mind of Christ," just like He promised. How I thank Him for His tender words spoken to me through you.

To my sweet Libby Brown: You had the prophetic vision for this book years before I ever got breast cancer. How I treasure our friendship!

To Katie Hamilton, my "Hope Floats" friend: How my life has been blessed through you! Thanks for inspiring and helping to write this devotion!

To all my dear, dear friends and prayer warriors on my e-mail list: Your prayers are such an integral part of my life and of this book, and I can never thank you enough.

To Elizabeth Ball, Acton Beard, Darlene McNeill, and Van Weston, my "wig party" buddies: How you encouraged me that day and throughout this breast cancer walk. I love you, dear friends. Thanks to Mary and Lee Callicutt, for making my hair cute at any length. You bring joy to so many!

To Ane DiVenere and all the members of The Open Door for Women Bible study: You loved me, listened to me, fed me, drove me, sat with me, and prayed for me. You healed me in ways you can't imagine.

To Bev Martin, Marie Durham, and all my other Christian "moms" who are so quick to say uplifting words to me: "May you who bless others be abundantly blessed" (Prov. 11:25).

To Dr. Craig Brackett, my friend and surgeon: Only God knows how many lives He has saved through the knowledge and expertise which He has given you. May He continue to guide and equip you in His service to the women of the Grand Strand and beyond, and bless your fabulous staff and family.

To the rest of my wonderful medical team, Dr. Darren Mullins, Dr. Eric Aguero, and Dr. Jack Hensel and their staffs: I thank God for your tender care and kind hearts. I pray for God's richest blessings on your practices and lives.

For their compassion and care of other chemotherapy maladies, I give thanks to Dr. Gayle Richmond, Dr. Laurence Ballou, Dr. Wright Skinner, Dr. Tom Cerasaro, and Dr. Jim Owens and to the outpatient care team at Georgetown Memorial Hospital. Special thanks to Phyllis, who saved me from a much-deserved stomach pumping. You never know how far little kindnesses will go.

To Jody Godby, for your editing and godly encouragement before the Florida Christian Writer's Conference, and to Kathy Eagen, for your willingness to type my manuscript when your plate was already full. I will continue to pray for God's blessings on you and your families.

# *Acknowledgments*

To Barbara Kois, my editor and new friend: Your gentleness even comes through the Internet! Thanks for all your help and encouragement.

To Christine St. Jacques, my wonderful project manager: We bonded from the very first phone call. Thank you for your consistently kind words, even when I made ridiculous suggestions.

To WinePress Publishing, for making this dream a reality.

To all my breast cancer buddies, who have shared so freely of their walk, their lives, and their hearts: We will forever be a sisterhood.

Finally, but most importantly, to my Lord and Savior: My name is on the cover, but You are the true Writer. Thank You for this new adventure!

# INTRODUCTION

> If you send them forward on their journey in a manner
> worthy of God, you will do well.
> —3 John 6 NKJV

THOSE WORDS WERE my marching orders. The instant I read them, I knew they were my divine directive and that realization excited and humbled me at the same time. While each of our walks takes a precise route, the manner in which we travel those roads is of the utmost importance to God.

As I traveled my pink journey these last few years, I wanted to make sure I was at least pretty on the inside, by His grace. So staying in the Word and near to my Lord served many purposes. It not only lessened my fears, but it also heightened my joy in Him, which, ultimately, showed on my face.

The strength and grace we need to walk this journey will only come by spending time in His presence. Regardless of our prognosis, or even of the ultimate outcome, His desire is for all of us to walk in faith, trusting Him to give us the shoes we will need for the path He has prepared for us. It is my prayer that *No Prissy Shoes* will encourage, console, and inspire you to walk your pink journey "in a manner worthy of God."

**—Linda Grabeman**

# NO PRISSY SHOES

*I* LOVE PRETTY shoes that are utterly gorgeous and totally impractical—what I call *prissy shoes*. If they have a bow, a flower, or glitter on them, great! If they are pink, even better! These shoes are fine for short periods, sunny days, and smoothly paved roads. I would love it if I could wear my prissy shoes for my whole life's journey—no stones on my path, no difficult cracks or crevices; just nice, smooth, straight highways of life.

But sometimes the course we are called to travel is neither smooth nor straight. Prissy shoes won't work there. If you are reading this devotional, you are more than likely walking a difficult road right now because of breast cancer.

In August 2006, I was also diagnosed with fairly advanced breast cancer. But God has been so faithful. Whenever my path has been hard, He has provided me with strong spiritual shoes, and that is the message of this book. Deuteronomy 29:5 says, "And I have led you forty years in the wilderness. Your clothes have not worn out on you, and your sandals have not worn out on your feet" (NKJV).

God has always been willing to provide for His people in adversity. He did it for the Israelites, and He will do it for you, if you will allow Him. He will gently take off your prissy shoes that served you well on the well-paved roads of prosperity, and replace them with strong, spiritual shoes for your grieving, uphill roads. And His shoes won't wear out on you!

Many years ago, I chose First Peter 3:15 to be the guiding verse for my life. "But sanctify Christ as Lord in your hearts, and always be ready to give a defense to everyone who asks you a reason for the hope that is in you" (NKJV). That verse is the passion for my life and the foundation for this book, which contains thirty-one devotions—one for each day of the month if you choose to read it that way. It is my prayer that as you read it you will experience God as the daily provider of strong spiritual shoes for your feet—victory shoes, overcoming shoes—for whatever stony paths you face.

Together, let's walk this breast cancer journey with hope—the hope that is found by sitting at the feet of Jesus and letting Him dress us with His choice shoes.

"If I were in your shoes, I'd go straight to God. I'd throw myself on the mercy of God. After all, he's famous for great and unexpected acts; there's no end to his surprises. He raises up the down-and-out, gives firm footing to those sinking in grief" (Job 5:8-9, 11).

"He lifted me out of the ditch, pulled me from deep mud. He stood me up on a solid rock to make sure I wouldn't slip" (Ps. 40:2).

God is strong, and he wants you strong. So take everything the Master has set out for you, well-made weapons of the best materials. And put them to use so you will be able to stand up to everything the Devil throws your way. This is no afternoon athletic contest that we'll walk away from and forget about in a couple of hours. Be prepared. You're up against far more than you can handle on your own. Take all the help you can get, every weapon God has issued, so that when it's all over but the shouting you'll still be on your feet.

—Ephesians 6:10-13

# FEELING FORSAKEN?

*I* WRITE NOTES on my hands. It works well for me because sometimes I lose the notes I've written on paper. My fourteen-year-old daughter taught me the wonder of this. I never forget these memos to myself, for the tablet they are written on is a part of me.

God knows this practice, too. He's been doing it for a very long time. So if you are feeling alone or forsaken right now, I have good news for you: God has engraved you on His hands.

If you doubt His love at this moment, you're not the first one! In Isaiah 49, God's people complain that He has forsaken and forgotten them. Do you know what His response is? He says that a mother might forget her infant, but he will *never* forget us, because we are written on His hands! He understands exactly what you are going through right now.

Throughout your busy days of mammograms or biopsies, radiation or just resting after chemotherapy, you aren't out of His thoughts for a second. He thinks about you constantly. Constantly.

As a mom, I can't get my mind around that one. I have three children, so I can't focus on just one of them all the time. Thoughts of the other two take over at some point. But God isn't like that. When you wake up, He's been thinking about you all night, longing to help and bless you. Doesn't that put a smile on your face?

I am, Lord willing, all done with my breast cancer surgeries. But all I have to do is glance at my chest and my side to remind myself of those days and all they entailed. Jesus has similar remembrances etched upon His body—on His hands, His feet, and His side. A look at any part of His glorified person reminds Him of what He endured for us. He has never forsaken us, and He never will. After keeping His promises a hundred times, will He not keep them the hundred and first time? For this reason, it is incomprehensible to think that in the midst of our struggles now He has forgotten us!

On one of the days you felt the lowest, you might have said, "I don't get it. God has left me. My Master has forgotten I even exist." If you have ever felt like God has left you, then make these next verses your own and hear once again God's answer to your loneliness:

"Can a mother forget the infant at her breast, walk away from the baby she bore? But even if mothers forget, I'd never forget you—never. Look, I've written your name on the backs of my hands" (Isa. 49:15-16).

I'm an open book to you; even from a distance, you know what I'm thinking. You know when I leave and when I get back; I'm never out of your sight. You know everything I'm going to say before I start the first sentence. I look behind me and you're there, then up ahead and you're there, too—your reassuring presence, coming and going. This is too much, too wonderful—I can't take it all in! You know me inside and out, you know every bone in my body; you know exactly how I was made, bit by bit, how I was sculpted from nothing into something. Like an open book, you watched me grow from conception to birth; all the stages of my life were spread out before you. The days of my life all prepared before I'd even lived one day. Your thoughts—how rare, how beautiful! God, I'll never comprehend them! I couldn't even begin to count them—any more than I could count the sand of the sea.

—Psalms 139:1-6, 13-18

# TO THE MAX

*I* HAD JUST spent the past week poring over Latin terms with my eighth grade daughter. It was exam week, and her stack of flash cards was overwhelming! I guess I had "good, better, and best" on my mind when I read Hebrews 7:24-25 in the Amplified Bible, for God gave me a new appreciation of the weightiness of these superlative words: unchangeably, forever, uttermost, always.

"But He holds His priesthood unchangeably, because He lives on forever. Therefore He is able also to save to the uttermost (completely, perfectly, finally, and for all time and eternity) those who come to God through Him, since He is always living to make petition to God *and* intercede with Him *and* intervene for them" (Heb. 7:24-25 AB).

What more could we ask for than a Savior Who is always praying for us and always planning good for us? He is unexcelled and unrivaled in His job as Advocate for us. What do you need Him to be for you today? Your world is shaken since your breast cancer diagnosis. Do you need a place of refuge where you can stand firm? He promises to be your Rock, and He's good at it—remember, He made Gibraltar.

Are the reports from doctors breaking like waves over your head faster than you can catch your breath? He promises to be your anchor in the storm. You've got a lot of decisions to make. Maybe you just need an advisor today. His comprehension of any situation is so complete that Isaiah called Him the Wonderful Counselor. Whatever attribute or strength you require, He has it. For just like His Father proclaimed in Exodus, Jesus the Son calls Himself the "I AM." He understands that the grace we will need to make it through this day is a little different from what we longed for last week. He knows only too well how situations can change on a dime. The highs of one Sunday can descend to the pits the next Friday. He has lived that expanse of emotions, which makes Him very good at dealing with ours. He is just waiting to be in our corner, on our behalf, for whatever we need. All we have to do is ask. He is always listening.

Do you remember writing words starting with the letters of the alphabet for your parents or a friend when you were little, extolling their virtues and letting them know how precious they were to you? Contemplate all that Jesus longs to be for you today.

Thinking about this led me to find words for Jesus starting with each letter of the alphabet using the verses below, all from the New King James Version. He said, "I am your…"

| | | |
|---|---|---|
| A | Anchor | Hebrews 6:19 |
| B | Blessing | Psalms 3:8 |
| C | Comfort | 2 Corinthians 1:3 |
| D | Deliverance | Proverbs 21:31 |
| E | Eternal Life | 1 John 2:25 |
| F | Faithfulness | Psalms 119:90 |
| G | Grace | Titus 2:11 |
| H | High Priest | Hebrews 4:14-15 |
| I | Intercessor | Hebrews 7:25 |
| J | Justifier | Romans 3:26 |
| K | King | 1 Timothy 1:17 |
| L | Life Abundant | John 10:10 |
| M | Message | 1 Corinthians 1:18 |
| N | New Covenant | Matthew 26:28 |
| O | Overseer | 1 Peter 2:25 |
| P | Peace | John 16:33 |
| Q | Quiet | Zephaniah 3:17 |
| R | Rock | Psalms 61:2 |
| S | Shepherd | John 10:11 |

| T | Triumph | 2 Corinthians 2:14 |
| U | Understanding | 2 Timothy 2:7 |
| V | Victory | 1 Corinthians 15:57 |
| W | Wisdom | James 1:5 |
| X | Exaltation | Philippians 2:9 |
| Y | Yes! | 2 Corinthians 1:19 |
| Z | Zeal | Titus 2:14 |

# WHY ME?

*Y*OU ARE NOT the only one who has ever asked, "Why me?!" Moses said it a long time ago. Are you shocked? He really did. Listen. "Moses said to God, 'Why are you treating me this way? What did I ever do to you to deserve this?'" (Num. 11:11).

God didn't have to include that verse in His Holy Word. I believe He did it to show us that He understands our protests when we feel overly burdened. He understands our desire for a secure, prosperous, satisfying life.

But acknowledging our feelings does not always mean giving in to our desires. God would like us to be happy, but He is more interested in our being *holy*. So if discomfort or dis-ease will produce the results God ultimately wants in our lives, He allows them. God has three goals for each of us: to refine us, to test our faith, and to glorify Himself in our life's journey. God wants us to shine for Him, and if breast cancer brings out qualities never before apparent in our lives, then so be it. God has always set a very high value on faith, and faith that has not been tested is little faith. We each have strength of character we would never know without trials to bring it to light.

A crucial question must be answered in our hearts before we determine our response to God during our breast cancer journey. I had to wrestle with this question early in my journey when my prognosis kept getting worse and worse.

I had to ask myself, *Why do I love Him? Do I love Him for all the good things He can do for me or for Who He is, whether He does one more "good" thing for me, or not? Can I, like Job, affirm that my love for God is irrespective of my circumstances?*

Trials endured, whatever they may be, prove not only to God, but to ourselves, how strong our trust in Him is. That's the *joy* part of the trial—learning that even in the midst of hard experiences, our faith stands. Even when we have to walk through difficult, draining times in our lives, we still praise God. That brings its own quiet contentment—that we have remained true to the One Who is always faithful.

So after you ask, "Why me?!" ask yourself, "Why do I love Him?" That is the most crucial question. Here are some verses that helped me answer that all-important question:

"The worst of my fears has come true, what I've dreaded most has happened. My repose is shattered, my peace destroyed. No rest for me, ever—death had invaded life" (Job 3:25-26).

"What? Shall we accept [only] good at the hand of God and shall we not accept [also] misfortune and what is of a bad nature? In [spite of] all this, Job did not sin with his lips" (Job 2:10 AB).

"Remember every road that God led you on for those forty years in the wilderness, pushing you to your limits, testing you so that he would know what you were made of, whether you would keep his command-ments or not. So it's paramount that you keep the commandments of God, your God, walk down the roads he shows you and reverently respect him" (Deut. 8:2, 6).

"Pure gold put in the fire comes out if it *proved* pure, genuine faith put through this suffering comes out *proved* genuine. When Jesus wraps this all up, it's your faith, not your gold, that God will have on display as evidence of his victory" (1 Peter 1:7).

"But He knows the way that I take [He has concern for it, appreciates, and pays attention to it]. When He has tried me, I shall come forth as refined gold [pure and luminous]" (Job 23:10 AB).

"Blessed (happy, to be envied) is the man who is patient under trial *and* stands up under temptation, for when he has stood the test *and* been approved, he will receive [the victor's] crown of life which God has promised to those who love Him" (James 1:12 AB).

# GOD'S LOVE NOTES

*T*HEY WERE CALLED *CliffsNotes* when I went to school. But that ages me. Now they are called *SparkNotes*. How did any of us get through English classes without them?

Believe it or not, God put His own book summaries—mini-*Reader's Digest* versions, if you will—in various and sundry places in His Word. It is very helpful to remember these little treasures when you are too sick or too stressed to pick up the whole Book. They are the lunchbox handwritten reminders from a Father Who knows where we are and longs for us to know that He is with us there.

Some days during chemo, I didn't have the stomach or the energy to pick up my Bible. On those days, the "God's Notes" I knew in my head and my heart were my devotions. I want to give you one of those mini-stories as a string to put around your finger to remind you that you are loved and you are not alone.

In Eugene Peterson's, *A Long Obedience in the Same Direction*, he gives a great six-word summary for the entire Bible. God stands, God stoops, God stays.[1] God stands sovereign over all. God stoops to help us, right where we are, if we just call on Him, and God stays when everyone else leaves, no matter what.

In my favorite God Note, at the very beginning of the Israelites' difficult journey from Egypt to the Promised Land, God declares the same statements. They were powerful for the arduous trek then, and they are just as effective for our breast cancer journeys right now:

> And the Lord said, "I have surely seen the affliction of My people who are in Egypt, and have heard their cry because of their taskmasters *and* oppressors; for I know their sorrows *and* sufferings *and* trials. And I have come down to deliver them out of the hand *and* power of the Egyptians and to bring them up out of that land to a land good and large…[a land of plenty]."
>
> —Exodus 3:7-8 AB

God sees, God hears, God knows, and God has come down. This God's Note is His love note for you during your difficult journey, just as it was for His people in ancient times. His heart and His power are still the same, and He longs to give meaning to your pink journey by using it to draw you into a deeper, more intimate relationship with Him.

Will you let Him do this? If so, then make these verses your own. Put your name and your specific problem in the blanks, and receive the message of the Bible in a new and more profound way. It is God's love note to you, written for all time!

> And the Lord said, "I have surely seen the affliction of (your name) in (your location), and I have heard your cry because of (your particular breast cancer); for I know your sorrows and sufferings and trials. And I have come down to deliver you out of the hand and power of (your breast cancer) and to bring you up out of that land to a land good and large, a land of plenty.
>
> —Exodus 3:7-8 AB

# THE GARDENER?

*A*S I READ from the book of John, I had never seen these words before, "Jesus spoke to her, 'Woman, why do you weep? Who are you looking for?' She, *thinking that he was the gardener*, said 'Mister, if you took him, tell me where you put him so I can care for him'" (John 20:15).

It is early Easter morning. Mary Magdalene has gone to the tomb of Jesus and found it empty. She stands outside of the grave, crying, when she sees Jesus. I was familiar with that part. But what I had never noticed before was "thinking that he was the gardener." Why in the world would she think He was the gardener?

If we go back one chapter we'll get our answer: "There was a garden near the place he was crucified, and in the garden a new tomb in which no one had yet been placed. So...they placed Jesus in it" (John 19:41, 42).

Mary thought Jesus was the gardener because He had been buried in a *garden*! Let's think about God and gardens. He designed a garden named Eden; He was betrayed in a garden named Gethsemane, and now He is buried and raised again in yet another garden. I think God *likes* gardens! But He doesn't just like gardens...listen to these verses:

"I will always show you where to go. I'll give you a full life in the emptiest of places. You'll be like a well-watered garden, a gurgling spring that never runs dry" (Isa. 58:11).

"They shall come and sing aloud on the height of Zion and shall flow together *and* be radiant with joy over the goodness of the Lord....

And their life shall be like a watered garden and they shall not sorrow *or* languish any more at all" (Jer. 31:12 AB).

God thinks *we* are His garden! That makes Him the Gardener! And He has quite a green thumb! He loves to bring beauty into barren places.

Being serene and calm while we walk through breast cancer seems like an elusive dream, but I can tell you from firsthand experience that God can make that happen. We just need to ask Jesus to tend our hearts and make them into a well-watered garden that's not afraid of the heat or drought.

Will you do that right now? Will you trust your wilderness places to the One Who can make them into His garden? Then make this verse your prayer: "God, pick up the pieces. Put me back together again. You are my praise" (Jer. 17:14).

These verses are also helpful for the times in the wilderness:

"God sent me to announce the year of his grace…and to comfort all who mourn, to care for the needs of all who mourn…give them bouquets of roses instead of ashes, messages of joy instead of news of doom, a praising heart instead of a languid spirit.

Rename them 'Oaks of Righteousness,' planted by God to display his glory" (Isa. 61:2-3).

"For the Lord will comfort [your name]. He will comfort all her waste places. And He will make her wilderness like Eden, and her desert like the garden of the Lord. Joy and gladness will be found in her, thanksgiving and the voice of song *or* instrument of praise" (Isa. 51:3 AB).

Walking this breast cancer journey brings mourning and lots of news of doom. God wants us to know His message of joy. He wants us to have praising hearts. And only He can take the places where we feel all alone and walking in a wilderness and turn them into Eden. But we must trust the overgrown or dry parts of our life's garden to His care. When we do, here's His promise:

"Blessed is the man who trusts me, God, the woman who sticks with God. They're like trees replanted in Eden, putting down roots near the rivers—never a worry through the hottest of summers, never dropping a leaf, serene and calm through droughts, bearing fresh fruit every season" (Jer. 17:7-8).

# TENDED

*M*Y HUSBAND AND I have a deal. He works in our yard, making the shrubs and trees look beautiful, and I take care of all the large flower pots on our front and back decks. We have a pond in our backyard, which we use to irrigate our grass and plants because coastal South Carolina summers can get very hot and dry. Without that water, everything would die. I love our yard all year long, but I especially enjoy it at Easter because it is the loveliest then. By then, my husband has sawed off and hauled away all the dead limbs and has meticulously pruned each tree to a beautiful shape. The azaleas and tulip magnolias are in bloom; my flower pots brim over with spring bulbs and annuals, and all the beds are adorned with a fresh cover of pine straw.

If we are God's garden, we need to be tended and watered too, and how graciously God does that! He wants the garden of our hearts to be "Easter pretty" all year long. There is no doubt that breast cancer is an exhausting, scary, and painful trip. But the One Who has designed every bend and curve of the route wants to tidy us up and deck us out, spiritually. But you are not going to believe the hoe He wants to use to spiff us up—forgiveness! Are you shaking your head "no" at me? If so, let me ask you a question: Who comes to mind when I say the word *forgive*? Is it someone whom you hurt with words that never should have been said? Or possibly someone who wounded your heart long ago? You know what I mean—nothing traumatic, just those tapes that play over and over in your mind that you wish wouldn't.

Let me tell you the most amazing thing that happened to me about six months before I began walking this breast cancer road. It was almost as if God was lightening my plate, knowing what would be on it shortly. I was introduced to the concept of intensive prayer by a friend. (Intensive prayer is simply a time set apart for prayer and stillness before the Lord, lifting up any specific hurts or situations to Him.) I knew that her life had taken some very difficult roads, but the joy on her face was unmistakable.

I went for prayer with her and a friend. We settled down to pray, and she invited the Holy Spirit to come and minister to me. She told me to let her know if I heard any words from the Lord or saw any pictures in my mind during our time of prayer.

After a few minutes of stillness before the Lord, a very vivid scene came to my mind. I was standing at a dump, where trash and yard debris lay piled all around. Jesus was right by my side. We were both looking at a huge pile of trash in a heap, burning.

Jesus said to me, "This is all the garbage and junk that has collected in your heart, and I am burning it for you to get rid of it." But the best part of that entire scene was Jesus' voice when He said those words—there was no condemnation in His statement, only love. I basked in the glow of that healing and freedom for a long time.

Jesus understands how weighed down we get with words and actions that break our hearts and steal our joy. He wants to heal those places—sins we have committed and those done to us—all that trash and debris from the garden of our hearts. He wants to be the garbage man. Many things besides breast cancer can cause us pain. So come, let God spruce up your garden. He is the Master Gardener. Those rotten limbs of words-wished-said and decaying debris of words-wished-never-said have choked out new green growth for too long. Jesus wants to burn them for you. He longs to do it for your sake. He also wants to do it for all those who will see your beautiful, tended heart garden along the way, and ask you Who your Gardener is. When they do, make sure you tell them it's Jesus!

I will make a fresh start with [insert your name].

[She'll] burst into bloom like a crocus in the spring.
[She'll] put down deep oak tree roots,
[She'll] become a forest of oaks!
[She'll] become splendid—like a giant sequoia,
(her) fragrance like a grove of cedars!
Those who live near [her] will be blessed by [her],
Be blessed and prosper, like golden grain.
Everyone will be talking about them,
Spreading their fame as the vintage children of God.
                    —Hosea 14:4-7, paraphrase by author

I am the Real Vine and my Father is the Farmer.
He cuts off every branch of me that doesn't bear grapes.
And every branch that is grape-bearing he prunes back
so it will bear even more. In the same way that a branch
can't bear grapes by itself but only by being joined to the vine,
You can't bear fruit unless you are joined with me. I
am the Vine, you are the branches. When you're joined with
me and I with you, the relation intimate and organic, the
harvest is sure to be abundant. This is how my Father
shows who he is—when you produce grapes, when you
mature as my disciples.
                              —John 15:1-2, 4-5, 7-8

"From the Water-of-Life Well I give freely to the thirsty" (Rev.
21:6).

# POST OFFICE CONVERSATIONS AND OTHER MISHAPS

*T*HICK SKIN. PRAY for it because, I promise, you'll need it! Right off the bat you need it for all the undressing, sitting naked from the waist up, and poking and prodding you have to endure! That's hard enough. But beyond the physical annoyances that just naturally go with breast cancer, you also have to brace yourself for the emotional exasperations that can make you crazy! So before you read any farther, I want to state in defense of all the insensitive, asinine statements that people will say to you—they don't mean it!

I learned that lesson in my first week after my diagnosis. I live in a fairly small southern town, and I've lived there nearly thirty years. So word of my breast cancer got around pretty quickly. I was in the post office and ran into an acquaintance. Here's a paraphrase of the conversation: "I'm sorry you have breast cancer. My (relative—I forget who) had breast cancer. She had chemotherapy and it helped. But later on, the cancer came back and she died. Good luck!"

Just punch me in the stomach, ma'am! But God is good, and He gave me enough of a sense of humor to laugh to myself as she walked away. Then, to keep me from being judgmental, He also reminded me of the times when I had said really stupid things to people. So instead of being angry at her insensitive words, I prayed for her embarrassment when she inevitably said to herself, "Why did I say that?"

But there is another group of people who will also hurt your feelings, and those are the ones from whom a sympathetic statement would be expected because they know you at least that well. Unfortunately, though, they are so uncomfortable with the subject of breast cancer, or are not great conversationalists to begin with, that they choose instead to remain silent. Ouch! Believe me, they are not deliberately trying to hurt your feelings—they just don't know what to say. Stupid words, or no words—I don't know which do more harm.

A month or so after my fun post office visit, our family decided to go to a popular local restaurant for dinner. It was early fall with gorgeous weather, so we ate on the outside deck. A great band was playing, so after we finished our meal, we joined the hundred or so people just standing around listening to the music. I was feeling horribly self-conscious because of this new "do" on my head (my wig), so my nerves were a little jittery anyway, but this next calamity just about did me in! I can laugh about it now, but at the time, it was very traumatic.

A sweet friend of ours came by to greet my husband and me, and in her excitement to see me, grabbed my face, and accidentally pulled my wig partially off of my head! We were both mortified. Like I said, pray for thick skin. (Now some breast cancer patients proudly wear bandanas or even go bald, and I stand in awe of them. I couldn't do that.)

Then came the "boob blunders." The first one was really a challenge because of the timing, but I survived. The very day that my bandages were removed from my first mastectomy and I could clearly see that I only had one breast, the *Sports Illustrated* swimsuit edition arrived in the mail. I made my husband take it out of the house. Later on in the process, there were days when I thought I looked so cute only to look down and see that my little "pillow" that was to take the place of my right breast had migrated to the center of my chest. You just have to have a sense of humor.

So for all these types of days and for all the others that will try your soul, I include these Bible verses for comfort and encouragement. Each of us has our own horror stories to tell, but with time, they all take on a comical feel. Just pray for God's thick-soled shoes of grace to walk you through these briars and thorns without too many scrapes. "And be not grieved *and* depressed, for the joy of the Lord is your strength *and* stronghold" (Neh. 8:10 AB).

"We pray that you'll have the strength to stick it out over the long haul—not the grim strength of gritting your teeth but the glory strength God gives. It is strength that endures the unendurable and spills over into joy, thanking the Father who makes us strong enough to take part in everything bright and beautiful that he has for us" (Col. 1:10-12).

"Take the old prophets as your mentors. They put up with anything, went through everything, and never once quit, all the time honoring God. What a gift life is to those who stay the course! You've heard, of course, of Job's staying power, and you know how God brought it all together for him at the end. That's because God cares, cares right down to the last detail" (James 5:10-11).

"Love never gives up. Doesn't fly off the handle, doesn't keep score of the sins of others, puts up with anything, trusts God always, always looks for the best, never looks back but keeps going to the end" (1 Cor. 13:4-7).

# LIAR, LIAR, PANTS ON FIRE!

*G*ET READY BECAUSE he's coming! No, I'm not talking about Santa Claus, I'm talking about Satan—with his arsenal of dirty bombs to launch at you when you are alone and scared and tired. He'll insinuate, intimidate, and downright deceive you to discourage and dissuade you from the truth you should know—that Jesus is *with* you, that He *loves* you, and that He will do *good* for you, even on your "pink" journey.

I learned the deceitfulness of the devil in the first week of my cancer walk. When my surgeon called me with the results of the mammogram, I asked him which breast looked bad. He laughed and said that he had seen so many mammograms recently, but he *thought* it was the left one. Immediately the old accuser started with his lies!

"Linda," he said, "you know that your left breast is the one closest to your heart. *You* have brought this breast cancer on yourself because of all the anger and resentment and pain which you have ever had in your heart! It is your fault that you have cancer!"

Wow! He really was living up to his reputation in Revelation 12:10 as "the accuser of the brethren"! But the truth was revealed the next day when I found out that it was the *right* breast! I almost laughed out loud in my doctor's office, but I was afraid they'd think I was crazy.

Let's get very clear about Satan's ways and his wiles because if you don't know the truth about him, you'll certainly fall for his lies. First, you need to know who and what this father of lies is. You also need to know what he isn't. He is a created being, so he is not eternal—he has not lived forever, like God. (Hallelujah on that one—we're not going to have to deal with him forever!) He is also not omniscient. He does not know our futures, only our pasts. (But he's a pro at that, and he'll bring it up to us again and again!) Third, he is not omnipresent. He can only be at one place at a time. (He needs all the other fallen angels to help him out.)

Finally, he is not omnipotent. God actively restrains Satan, and everything he does has to be approved by God. (However, God promises that He will not allow us to be tempted beyond what we can bear.)

Now that we know who he is and what he does, we can recognize his slimy fingerprints when we feel discouraged or doubtful, dismayed, desperate, depressed, or discontented. All those "D" words come straight from the devil, as his calling cards from hell. Breast cancer brings its own satchel of "downers," but Satan can intensify them to make us feel lower than low.

Whenever we sink into his "pits" we need to remember who is leading us there, and Who will rescue us! If that is where you are right now, ask the One Who often said "Rise" to those whom He healed to help you "rise" out of Satan's doom and gloom. Can't you feel His hand lifting you up?

Satan is *not* eternal:

You were the anointed cherub. I placed you on the mountain of God. From the day of your creation you were sheer perfection… and then imperfection—evil!—was detected in you.

I threw you, disgraced, off the mountain of God. I threw you out—you, the anointed angel-cherub. Your beauty went to your head.

—Ezekiel 28:12-17

Satan is *not* omniscient (all-knowing):

(Satan said), "But what do you think would happen if you reached down and took away everything that is his (Job)? He'd curse you right to your face, that's what."

24

Job got to his feet, ripped his robe, shaved his head, then fell to the ground and worshipped: Naked I came from my mother's womb, naked I'll return to the womb of the earth. God gives, God takes. God's name be ever blessed. Not once through all this did Job sin, not once did he blame God.

—Job 1:11, 20-22

Satan is *not* omnipresent or omnipotent: "One day when the angels came to report to God, Satan, who was the Designated Accuser, came along with them. God singled out Satan and said, 'What have you been up to?' Satan answered God, 'Going here and there, checking things out on earth'" (Job 1:6-7).

"So let God work his will in you. Yell a loud *no* to the devil and watch him scamper. Say a quiet *yes* to God and he'll be there in no time" (James 4:7-8).

Keep a cool head. Stay alert. The devil is poised to pounce, and would like nothing better than to catch you napping. Keep your guard up. You're not the only one plunged into these hard times. It's the same with Christians all over the world. So keep a firm grip on the faith. The suffering won't last forever. It won't be long before this generous God who has great plans for us in Christ—eternal and glorious plans they are!—will have you put together and on your feet for good. He gets the last word; yes, he does.

—1 Peter 5:8-11

# WHO SAYS?

/T WAS TIME to declare war. Satan had tried to ambush me one too many times, and I was mad! My days were all running together with biopsies, MRIs, CT scans, and bone scans. But tonight was the last straw! I had an MRI yesterday, which my surgeon, who is a dear friend of mine, happily said showed a smaller area of disease than my mammogram had.

Tonight he called me to say that he would be at my house in ten minutes. He looked absolutely distraught when he arrived. He sat on our sofa and told me that he had re-examined my MRI with the radiologists, and they had decided that the area was larger than they had originally thought, *and* there was abnormal activity in my left breast, too!

Then he looked right at me and said, "Linda, I just wanted to give you some *hope!*" This precious man, whom God had anointed and called to do wonderful healing work on thousands of women with breast cancer, was agonizing over the news he had to give me. But I was determined to let him know exactly where I stand, spiritually, in this journey. I said, just as seriously, in response, "You are not the *source* of my hope!" For even though the men reviewing my case had the letters M.D. after their names, they were mortals, just like me.

The next day, my husband and I met him in his office, and he told us over and over, "I am very, very worried." As we left, he gave me a big pink folder about breast cancer. We got in our car, and I said to my husband, "I am not going to be stupid about my disease, but I am *not* going to spend my days becoming an expert on breast cancer! I am going to spend my days reading my Bible and immersing myself in God's Truth, not the "facts" as the world sees them." Thankfully, he agreed. The war was on—truth vs. facts.

I wrote this in my journal:

"Lord, help me to keep my eyes on You! Let me never look at the 'giants' in my life right now. Give me a courageous heart, like David, to see, instead of the 'giant' of breast cancer, Your omnipotent, omniscient, Almighty hand at work in my life. When I contemplate Who is ordaining and controlling all the events of this past month, I am not afraid because I know You to be a trustworthy God. Keep reminding me of that, Lord. Give me new remembrances to keep the fire of my faith fueled up."

No matter what the "facts" are, keep looking to the Truth. (Remember John 17:17—the Word is Truth.) He is your hope, and He is worthy of your trust. If you have been overwhelmed lately with "facts," take a few minutes now to sit with the One Who is "the way, the truth, and the life" (John 14:6). He'll never lead you down a wrong path.

As we read in Proverbs 1:33, "First, pay attention to me, and then relax. Now you can take it easy—you're in good hands."

I'll never forget the trouble, the utter lostness, the taste of ashes, the poison I've swallowed. I remember it all—oh, how well I remember— the feeling of hitting the bottom. But there's one other thing I remember, and remembering, I keep a grip on hope. God's loyal love couldn't have run out, his merciful love couldn't have dried up. They're created new every morning. How great is your faithfulness! I'm sticking with God (I say it over and over), He's all I've got left. God proves to be good to the man who patiently waits, to the woman who diligently seeks. It is a good thing to quietly hope, quietly hope for help from God.

—Lamentations 3:19-26

# WHAT IF?

*W*HAT IF? THEY are the most distressing words in the English language. Charles Haddon Spurgeon said it well (he always does) when he wrote, "Ifs, buts, and perhapses are sure murderers of peace and comfort."[2] Haven't you found that to be true in your own life? When you start projecting into your future, especially on this particular journey, your peace is extinguished and your fears blaze like a bonfire! I hear it often from breast cancer sisters. I've been down that road myself. *What if chemo didn't get it all? What if my cancer comes back, now that my chemo is over? What if I have another bad mammogram?*

We place our faith in the wrong things—in the very smart, yet not infallible doctors; in the rigorous, but not perfected chemotherapy; in the skilled, yet only human hands of the surgeons.

God gave me the best object lesson on the reality of His presence a few years ago on a family vacation. We were in Costa Rica, preparing to zip line through the trees (very high up in the trees!) after a nerve-racking bus ride up goat path roads. It was very important to my three children that we do this as a family, so I reluctantly agreed. Never having been a fan of high places, I quietly put on my harness as they all excitedly bantered about how "cool" this was. But when the time came for our group to walk out to the jumping-off platform, I absolutely fell apart. My husband and children stood dumbfounded (and mortified) as, panic-stricken, I wailed these words, *"I can't do this!"*

Never in my life have I ever been that frightened. But then I heard this kind, softly spoken reply, "It's okay, I'll go with you and I'll carry you." It was the guide speaking. He said, "You let me hold you, and we'll go across together."

I was still petrified, but now I had someone who was experienced on the course as my navigator. I knew he wouldn't do anything to jeopardize his own life, so he could be trusted to protect mine, too. I did it, and not just once, either. The course involved nine different zip lines, and once you started, there was no turning back. My blood pressure lowered just a little bit during each section of the aerial path, and by the end, I actually almost had fun!

But the significance of that picture with a purpose didn't hit me until I was taking a quiet walk a few weeks later. God brought that experience to my mind and revealed to my heart that zip lining through the jungle with a guide was a picture of the last few years of my life. As I had traversed the steep, treacherous breast cancer road, He had been my Guide, and He had carried me! I felt cherished and protected.

As I contemplated all the events that had made up my pink path, I realized that all of my anticipated calamities either had never occurred, or by God's grace, together we had walked through them. Every new obstacle on this course presents the same option to us. We can either choose to take the road wrought with fears and ominous misgivings—the path devised and delighted in by the devil himself. Or we can choose to take the God-road, which follows the One Who is not only Companion, but Comforter, Counselor, and Conqueror, too. We can go down that detour which is a tortuous, haunted back road where fog and dark clouds hide the sun. Or we can choose to walk on the road illuminated by the Light of the World, the most capable and experienced Guide.

So the next time Satan tries to spook you with his slanderous "What if?" answer him back with your own adage—"*So what!*" Because whatever happens, God will be there, and God will carry you if you let Him! Thanks be to God!

I've picked you. I haven't dropped you. Don't panic. I'm with you.
There's no need to fear for I'm your God. I'll give you strength.
I'll help you. I'll hold you steady, keep a firm grip on you.

That's right. Because I, your GOD, have a firm grip on you and I'm not letting go. I'm telling you "Don't panic. I'm right here to help you."

—Isaiah 41:9-10, 13

I'm still in your presence, but you've taken my hand.
You wisely and tenderly lead me, and then you bless me.
You're all I want in heaven! You're all I want on earth!
When my skin sags and my bones get brittle, GOD is
rock-firm and faithful. Look! Those who left you are
falling apart! Deserters, they'll never be heard from
again. But I'm in the very presence of God—oh,
how refreshing it is! I've made Lord GOD my home.
God, I'm telling the world what you do.

—Psalms 73:23-28

I love you, GOD—you make me strong. GOD is bedrock
under my feet, the castle in which I live, my rescuing knight.
My God—the high crag where I run for dear life, hiding
behind the boulders, safe in the granite hideout.
I sing to God, the Praise-Lofty, and find myself safe and saved.

—Psalms 18:1-3

Peace I leave with you; My [own] peace I now give
*and* bequeath to you. Not as the world gives do I give
to you. Do not let your hearts be troubled, neither let
them be afraid. [Stop allowing yourselves to be agitated
and disturbed; and do not permit yourselves to be
fearful and intimidated and cowardly and unsettled].

—John 14:27 AB

And let the peace (soul harmony which comes) from Christ
rule (act as umpire continually) in your hearts [deciding
and settling with finality all questions that arise in your
minds, in that peaceful state] to which as [members of
Christ's] one body you were also called [to live]. And be
thankful (appreciative), [giving praise to God always].

—Colossians 3:15 AB

# GOD'S GPS

*I*T WAS MY first experience with a Global Positioning System. How I thank the designer of this device that is so vital to those of us who are directionally challenged! I was driving my daughter to a camp in the mountains, and I rarely drive far from home (it's just not safe!) so this guidance system meant the difference between arriving safely and being irretrievably lost somewhere in the boondocks.

When we began the trip, we thought we would have smooth sailing and an easy arrival at our destination. As we drove, however, our frustration with this little contraption grew. It only informed us of our present path with no "big picture" and no preview of how we would get to our journey's end. This sketchy understanding of the exact path we would take caused us increasing anxiety.

We yelled at the device that wouldn't give us the information, but instead just kept saying, "Go forward," which we did with not the greatest attitudes. Then, with no hint or warning, suddenly the screen showed our desired goal. We were there! "It" knew all along that we were headed in just the right direction. My daughter and I had spent much time on the cell phone with our friends at the camp, deriding the navigational aid and bemoaning our supposed disorientation. We thought we were alone, lost, and helpless because of our lack of faith in our electronic mapmaker. But our twists and turns were all actually designed—not just random wanderings.

In our lives, we grumble when we think our Guide is leading us on a path too steep or full of briers. Our backs ache, our feet scream, and we are far past weary. We have cast off our prissy shoes and feel like what we need right now is a pair of combat boots for this journey. But our Pacesetter knows our frame, that we are dust. If any other route were better for us, He would have chosen it. He knows the very best trail for us to take and, though ever-patient with our complaints, He longs for us to trust His direction. So today, let's ask Him to help us follow more faithfully, wherever He leads. And since He alone knows the terrain of the path we will take today, let's ask Him for the right shoes, too. It will make the road much easier to walk.

Will you ask Him to help you follow more faithfully, wherever He leads? He is the only road map we need for life's journey, and He is the destination, too.

Here are some of my favorite verses that illustrate this:

"God is fair and just; He corrects the misdirected, sends them in the right direction. From now on every road you travel will take you to GOD. Follow the Covenant signs; Read the charted directions" (Ps. 25:8, 10).

"You're my cave to hide in, my cliff to climb. Be my safe leader, be my true mountain guide. Free me from hidden traps; I want to hide in you. I've put my life in your hands. You won't drop me, you'll never let me down" (Ps. 31:3-5).

"I'll take the hand of those who don't know the way, who can't see where they're going. I'll be a personal guide to them, directing them through unknown country. I'll be right there to show them what roads to take, make sure they don't fall into the ditch. These are the things I'll be doing for them—sticking with them, not leaving them for a minute" (Isa. 42:16).

"For the Lord will go before you, and the God of Israel will be your rear guard" (Isa. 52:12 AB).

# KNIT ONE, PURL ONE

*C*ONFUSED? WONDERING WHAT in the world God is doing? Guess what—you've got good company. The disciples didn't understand Jesus when He walked this earth either. He even talked to them about it. Here's what He said as He sat with them at the Last Supper: "You don't understand now what I am doing, but it will be clear enough to you later" (John 13:7).

The sweet thing about their relationship was that Jesus understood their misunderstanding. He knew that one day they would comprehend His big plan. One day we will too. But until then, we just have to trust Him. I love this quote from A. W. Tozer: "To the child of God, there is no such thing as an accident. He travels in an appointed way... Accidents may indeed appear to befall him and misfortune stalk his way; but these evils will be so in appearance only and will seem evils only because he cannot read the secret script of God's hidden providences."[3]

A wise friend named Acton said something to me that has colored my view of this whole breast cancer journey. When I told her my diagnosis, she said, "It's not all about you, Linda." *It's not all about you.* Yes, we are women with breast cancer. But we are also daughters, friends, probably mothers, and possibly sisters. Our lives intersect many other lives, and God may be using our breast cancer walk to touch them in a specific way. His perspective is always so much larger than ours, and His bottom line is our hearts, not our happiness. Three years into my pink journey, I can see some of God's handiwork in this path He has chosen for me.

But even as I walked it, He gave me assurances that this was not just a whim on His part, but rather a very skillfully designed itinerary for many people besides me. During prayer with others one day, I very clearly saw His divine hands knitting, stitch by stitch. As I talked to a friend about this visual prayer, we reflected on the fact that sometimes in knitting, stitches get dropped, causing a hole in the piece. That's where God comes in with His heavenly needles and picks up the stitches and mends the hole.

I thought about the "holes" in my personal life and in my relationships with others, and how God had blessed them through my breast cancer. My children, who had always had a stay-at-home mom ready at their beck and call, had matured into more self-reliant teenagers. Outside our immediate family, God touched others' lives, too. He made friends out of mere acquaintances and deep friendships out of casual ones. He drew those who rarely ever thought about Him to prayer; and those who love Him even closer to Him. And last, but not least, He finally changed my sweet, sweet husband into a hand-holder. (I had been trying to teach him that for twenty-four years!) Now how could I selfishly wish that God would have excluded me from this difficult walk when He was going to work in the lives of so many others because of it? I couldn't. So put on your God-glasses and just believe that He is going to bring blessings out of this terrible disease—for you and for others. It's how He works, all the time.

> I don't think the way you think.
> The way you work isn't the way I work.
> God's Decree.
> For as the sky soars high above earth,
> so the way I work surpasses the way you work,
> and the way I think is beyond the way you think.
> Just as rain and snow descend from the skies
> and don't go back until they've watered the earth,
> Doing their work of making things grow and blossom,
> producing seed for farmers and food for the hungry,
> So will the words that come out of my mouth

not come back empty-handed.
They'll do the work I sent them to do,
they'll complete the assignment I gave them.

—Isaiah 55:8-11

Long before he laid down earth's foundations, he
had us in mind, had settled on us as the focus of
his love, to be made whole and holy by his love.
He set it all out before us in Christ, a long-range
plan in which everything would be brought together
and summed up in him, everything in deepest
heaven, everything on planet earth. It's in Christ that
we find out who we are and what we are living for.
Long before we first heard of Christ and got our hopes up,
he had his eye on us, had designs on us for glorious
living, part of the overall purpose he is working out in
everything and everyone.

—Ephesians 1:3-4, 10-12

"I've told you all this so that trusting me, you will be unshakeable
and assured, deeply at peace. In this godless world you will continue
to experience difficulties. But take heart! I've conquered the world."
(John 16:32-33)

# ON HIM

*I*T HAD BEEN a very difficult few weeks. My fourth chemotherapy had hit me like a ton of bricks, and I was just beginning to get my shaky legs to hold me when another blast came. My oldest son, Christian, was hospitalized for six days when his lung spontaneously collapsed, a fairly common thing for tall, thin teenage boys. As I spent those long, sleepless nights in the hospital with him, I would have gladly taken countless more chemotherapies rather than watch my precious child suffer. It was a painful time for me, but I just had to trust him to the Lord, and then wait for Him to bring healing in His way and His time.

Waiting. You do a lot of that when you walk this breast cancer journey. Wait for the results of the mammogram, wait for the ultrasound and the biopsy and the phone call regarding the chemotherapy. Wait, wait, and wait. It is hard and it is scary. That's the bad news. The good news is this—God knows. He knows right where you are. He has anticipated it since the dawn of time, and He is right with you while you wait. He is with you and He is not empty-handed. He has come with a wonderful promise to soothe those nerves that are raw from waiting. Psalm 28:7 says, "My heart trusts in, relies on, *and* confidently leans on Him, and I am helped" (AB).

A similar verse was my lifeline when the road got especially rugged: "For since the beginning of the world men have not heard nor perceived by the ear, nor has the eye seen any God besides You Who acts for the one who waits for Him" (Isa. 64:4 NKJV). That verse gave me comfort

39

as I waited over and over during my journey. It gave me a deep, abiding peace to know that my ears couldn't hear enough and my eyes couldn't see enough to realize how much my God was acting on my behalf as I waited on Him.

The trick to it, though, is to wait *on Him.* That's very different from just waiting. Simply waiting for phone calls and results, diagnoses and procedures will make you crazy. It will consume your thoughts and rob your peace as it fills your days with dread. But waiting on Him is a different story altogether.

One particularly bleak night during Christian's recuperation, he asked me why I could trust the Lord so much easier than he could. With a smile, I reminded him that he was only seventeen years old, and I was over fifty. In all those extra years, God had proven Himself to be faithful so many times that I knew He was trustworthy. We still have to go through those rough places in our journeys, but we just know from experience that God will walk us through them, with whatever type of shoes we may need.

So don't simply wait. Wait on Him. Even during your pink travels God can do more good and bring more blessings than your eyes can ever see or your ears can ever hear. Take a moment now and search your heart for those places where you don't yet believe that God will act for you if you wait on Him. Then make these verses personal by inserting your name.

"And you shall know [with an acquaintance and understanding based on and grounded in personal experience] that I am the Lord; for they shall not be put to shame who wait for, look for, hope for, *and* expect me" (Isa. 49:23 AB).

Help, GOD—the bottom has fallen out of my life! Master, hear my cry for help! Listen hard! Open your ears! Listen to my cries for mercy. I pray to GOD—my life, a prayer—and wait for what he'll say and do. My life's on the line before God, my Lord, waiting and watching till morning, waiting and watching till morning. O [insert your name], wait and watch for GOD—with GOD's arrival, comes love, with GOD's arrival comes generous redemption.

—Psalms 130:1-2, 5-7

"So—who is like me? Who holds a candle to me?" says The Holy.

Look at the night skies: Who do you think made all this?

Who marches this army of stars out each night, counts them off, calls each by name—so magnificent! so powerful!—and never overlooks a single one?

Why would you ever complain, O [your name], or, whine, [your name] saying, "God has lost track of me. He doesn't care what happens to me"?

Don't you know anything? Haven't you been listening?

GOD doesn't come and go. God *lasts*. He's Creator of all you can see or imagine.

He doesn't get tired out, doesn't pause to catch his breath.

And he knows *everything*, inside and out.

He energizes those who get tired, gives fresh strength to dropouts.

For even young people tire and drop out, young folk in their prime stumble and fall.

But those who wait upon GOD get fresh strength. They spread their wings and soar like eagles, they run and don't get tired, they walk and don't lag behind.

—Isaiah 40:25-31

# FLAWLESS

*I* WAS LOOKING at some family pictures with my fourteen-year-old daughter, Chloe. She said, "My chin looks splotchy here. My hair looks frizzy; can't we take some new pictures?"

Listening to her, I saw myself again at age fourteen, noticing the things I would change about my appearance. To be completely honest, I saw myself at fifty-four, too! We often focus on our imperfections when we see ourselves, either in the mirror or in pictures. How profoundly different our eyesight is from that of our heavenly Father. We can easily recite a long list of imperfections in the way we look. He, on the other hand, thinks we are *flawless*.

The other day I ordered some accessories online. At the end of my shipping confirmation from a well-known retail store was this statement: "Thank you for shopping with _____. We hope you feel beautiful."

At first glance, that made me smile, but then it made me ponder. What if I hadn't ordered that animal print belt? Would I not feel as beautiful? Is a package from my favorite clothing store the basis of my sense of beauty? Without that too-cool belt, would I be ugly? And who determines whether I am lovely or not? Is it the person in the shipping department of a catalog, who will never lay eyes on me? Or, almost as bad, is it me? Because if my attractiveness is dependent on my self-analysis, then many days, I'm really lacking! But if I turn to the One Who formed me for my basis for beauty, everything changes. Here is what He thinks about us:

You're so beautiful, my darling, so beautiful...
You're beautiful from head to toe, my dear love, beautiful beyond
   compare, absolutely flawless.
You've captured my heart, dear friend.
You looked at me, and I fell in love.
One look my way and I was hopelessly in love!
                                        —Song of Songs 4:1, 7, 9


Two weeks after my chemo began, my hair started to fall out, and these excerpts are from two e-mails I sent: "On went my wig! Getting accustomed to it will be a journey in itself. Mirrors are not my best friend right now because I don't recognize the person that I see. So the next time you see me, I will look a little different, but I'm the same Linda on the inside!"

Later that month, I wrote,

God has been doing a wonderful healing in my HEART! This "losing your hair/wig thing" is not just a one-time adjustment. You have to deal with it EVERY day. God has been showing me how very different His idea of beauty is from the world's view and how many places in my own life I have bought into the world's lies. It has been a very sweet time of learning. But only a God Who has been turning the world upside down since His incarnation 2,000 years ago would teach me about true beauty by allowing every hair on my body to fall out!"

The prettiest makeup of all has always been the joy of the Lord. Make sure it is your foundation before you apply anything else! Then take off your prissy shoes, and gratefully replace them with His shoes of love for you. They'll make you feel *radiant*! In Ephesians 5:26-27, we read, "Christ's love makes the church whole. His words evoke her beauty. Everything he does and says is designed to bring the best out of her, dressing her in dazzling white silk, radiant with holiness."

"What matters is not your outward appearance—the styling of your hair, the jewelry you wear, the cut of your clothes—but your inner disposition. Cultivate inner beauty, the gentle, gracious kind that God delights in" (1 Peter 3:3-4).

# NEVER A "*NOW WHAT?*"

*T*HERE IS NO gentler teacher than Jesus. When He explains something, He uses the most easily understood examples, and He continues to give "for instances" until we get it. The summer after my chemotherapy and first mastectomy, He showed me the "width and length and depth and height" of His love for us. He didn't want me to miss the message, so He used vivid experiences in my life to illustrate.

In Proverbs 18:24 (AB) we read, "But there is a friend who sticks closer than a brother." Jesus is that kind of friend.

That summer He showed me how He *doesn't* love us. He doesn't love like I do—on again and off again. He made that abundantly clear through a cell phone conversation. I was at a radiology appointment when my brother called me. I greeted him and asked him how he was, to which he replied, "Oh, just fine and dandy," with a sarcastic tone. That comment didn't sit well with me since, in my mind, my days (for quite a long time) had been much more stressful than his could ever be. My very unloving response was, "*Now* what?!"

As I hung up, I clearly heard the Lord say to my heart, "Aren't you glad I never say '*Now* what?!' to you, Linda?" I humbly gave thanks for that truth.

But not only did the Lord want to impress upon me how He would *never* act; He also wanted to etch on my memory a vision of how He would *always* act. My oldest son, Christian, had gone to Jamaica on his first mission trip during the summer before his senior year in high school. Our family as well as friends from church anxiously awaited his team's arrival at the airport. Security required that we stand behind a certain point as they deplaned. My husband, daughter, younger son, Carey, and I were all on tiptoes to get a glimpse of Christian and the team. But as they came into view, Carey could not contain himself any longer. He pushed ahead of the crowd into the area marked "No Admittance" and tackled his brother with a giant bear hug!

Without a moment's hesitation, he unashamedly broke the rules and unreservedly showed his love for his brother. That is Jesus' heart for us, at all times and in all places!

These two snapshots of our Savior's love demonstrate the fact that He will never get tired of hearing about our trials and sorrows or our joys and cares. He is always interested, always compassionate, always ready to encourage and guide. And no matter how much we *think* He loves us, it is really so much more!

Take a moment right now and ask the Lord to impress on your heart the dimensions of His love for you, for that love is higher and deeper, wider and longer than you can ever comprehend. He promises us, "I've never quit loving you and never will. Expect love, love, and more love!" (Jer. 31:3).

So what do you think? With God on our side like this, how can we lose? If God doesn't hesitate to put everything on the line for us, embracing our condition and exposing himself to the worst by sending his own Son, is there anything else he wouldn't gladly and freely do for us? Do you think anyone is going to be able to drive a wedge between us and Christ's love for us? There is no way.

—Romans 8:31-32, 35

# GOD ISN'T A DRIVE-THROUGH

WHEN MY MIDDLE child, Carey, was much younger, he had what I called the "McDonald's mentality." He had been to the golden arches a few too many times, so when we took our family out to a nice "sit-down" restaurant, he got impatient and annoyed at how long it took. I think that all too often we have spiritual "McDonald's mentality." We're all too prone to settle for a "Jesus drive-through."

Breast cancer intensifies that "hurry up" attitude. Add doctor's appointments, hospital visits, and serious stress to an already crammed schedule and you've got the perfect recipe for a basket case! That's just what I was on the morning of October 26, 2006. I was five weeks into my chemotherapy, and I had a bald head (or rather, a bald body!), and I was beside myself. My precious friend, Alex, a retired bishop from west Tennessee and my spiritual mentor, called to check in on me, and I was fretting, to say the least!

But here is what had me so very upset—thank you notes! Satan had wound me in a tizzy over my ever-growing list of notes I knew I should write. But Jesus' tender, compassionate voice spoke through Alex, and he told me to lay down the notes and spend time with Him, so that I could hear His quiet voice over the discord of my world. I had let my "responsibilities" steal all my time and energy, and then I handed Jesus what was left—a drive-through visit from a weary, worn-out child. But thanks be to God, Jesus is always ready to take us back! Here's what He says to us:

"Look at me. I stand at the door. I knock. If you hear me call and open the door, I'll come right in and sit down to supper with you. Are your ears awake? Listen." (Rev. 3:20, 22).

It's all about opening the door to Him and shutting it to the world. The blessings of doing this are beyond measure for not only does Jesus promise that He will be with us, but also that He will eat with us. In our fast-paced world, though, we can't comprehend exactly what He means by eating with us (another reason we settle for Jesus drive-throughs).

Are you ready to spend some quality time with your Lord? Right now, ask Him to take off your prissy shoes and rub your hot, burning feet with His tender hands. Just close your eyes and rest in His presence. He wants to refresh you!

Here are some verses that give us insight into the depth of what He means by eating with us. Think of the disciples at the Last Supper. Not only did they have a meal with Jesus, reclining at the table with Him, but He also refreshed them by washing their feet (just think how nice getting your feet rubbed feels).

> [Jesus] got up from supper, took off His garments, and taking a [servant's] towel, He fastened it around His waist. Then He poured water into the washbasin and began to wash the disciples' feet and to wipe them with the [servant's] towel with which He was girded.
> —John 13:4-5 AB

And in Luke 12:37 we read:

> Blessed (happy, fortunate, and to be envied) are those servants whom the master finds awake *and* alert *and* watching when he comes. Truly I say to you, he will gird himself and have them recline at table and will come and serve them! (AB)

And in Acts 3:19, "Turn around *and* return [to God]...that times of refreshing (of recovering from the effects of heat, of reviving with fresh air) may come from the presence of the Lord" (AB).

Not only does Jesus want to feed us in our quiet times, He wants to refresh us. He wants us to feel loved and satisfied and restored. Does that sound good to anyone besides me? He knows that we are all prone to doing too much and running too fast. He knows our feet ache and our prissy shoes hurt. But He is quite the gentleman, so He just stands, waiting. Waiting for us to hear His voice, open the door and let Him dine with us—not the drive-through kind of eating, but really reclining with Him and being refreshed by Him.

It is my prayer that each of us gets so comfortable in His presence that we don't want to run off so quickly. And maybe over a lifetime, and through our breast cancer journey, we'll finally be able to say, like David did:

> When besieged, I'm calm as a baby.
> When all hell breaks loose, I'm collected and cool.
> I'm asking God for one thing, only one thing:
> To live with him in his house my whole life long.
> I'll contemplate his beauty; I'll study at his feet.
> That's the only quiet, secure place in a noisy world,
> The perfect getaway, far from the buzz of traffic.
> God holds me head and shoulders above all who try to pull me down.
> I'm headed for his place to offer anthems that will raise the roof!
> Already I'm singing God-songs; I'm making music to God.
> —Psalms 27:3-6

# JESUS CHICKS

*J*ESUS CHICKS. YOU may think this devotion is about motorcycle mommas, since I live twenty-five miles from Myrtle Beach, the Harley Davidson motorcycle Mecca. Actually, I am referring to some fantastic verses in Matthew 23, which say: "Oh, Jerusalem, Jerusalem… How often I wanted to gather your children together, as a hen gathers her chicks under her wings, but you were not willing! See! Your house is left to you desolate" (Matt. 23:37-38 NKJV).

When our lives are unraveling or nothing makes sense and we have no idea where to go, Jesus wants to gather us as His little chicks under His wings. If we are smart, we'll run right to that refuge whenever a storm approaches. But sometimes we are not as smart as baby chicks, and Jesus tells us where we will end up—our houses will be desolate.

I had a real picture of that desolation with my young daughter, Chloe, shortly after my diagnosis. I wrote this in my journal: "Chloe has been so distant and spending so much time in her own world. Tonight is my last night with hair. Tomorrow morning, I am going to get my head shaved and begin wearing my wig. (I have no desire to watch my hair fall out daily, so two weeks after beginning chemo, I have scheduled a 'wig party' appointment for myself and some girlfriends at my hairdresser's).

"As I put Chloe to sleep tonight, I asked her to feel my hair one more time, and she burst out crying! She said, 'Mommy, I can't believe you have breast cancer, and every time I think about it, I am shocked all over again! Every time you go for an MRI or chemotherapy, it hurts me so much!' We snuggled and prayed, hugged and talked for a long time. She cried and said that sometimes she was afraid I would die. Finally, she let it out! And all of a sudden, I had my darling daughter back! Thank You, Lord! She had been so estranged from me, and it hurt so much! What a relief!"

God wanted me to feel a speck of the pain He feels when we run *from* Him instead of dashing under His protective wings for cover. He understands all the places where we will need to be comforted, and He is ready and waiting to provide that solace. Then why don't we run to Him? Why is He so often our last resort when we are scared or hurting? He should be our first line of defense. Now, don't get me wrong. Husbands, sisters, mothers, and girlfriends provide fabulous support, but we're talking about unequalled, ultimate understanding and power here. Why don't we tap into it? Why don't we run to His loving, caring arms and let ourselves be wrapped in His love? He longs to comfort us. It's one of His names, you know, the Comforter, the Counselor. He aches to take our tear-stained faces and lift them up to see His tender, gentle gaze.

David understood this. He wrote in Psalm 3:3 that the Lord is "the One who lifts up my head" (NKJV). Paul understood it too, for he wrote to the Corinthians, "For even when we arrived in Macedonia, our bodies had no ease *or* rest, but we were oppressed in every way *and* afflicted at every turn—fighting *and* contentions without, dread *and* fears within [us]. But God, Who comforts *and* encourages *and* refreshes *and* cheers the depressed *and* the sinking, comforted *and* encouraged *and* refreshed *and* cheered us…" (2 Cor. 7:5-6 AB).

Paul tells about the stark realities of his life. He does not run and hide from his problems, trying to deny that they exist. He acknowledges them and then runs to Jesus with them, hiding in the cleft of the Rock. John, the beloved disciple, understood where to go when life's twists and turns had his head spinning. He laid his head on Jesus' bosom.

No matter what our problem is, the answer is the safety of His sanctuary. Will you bring your problems to Him now? Will you honestly pour out your heart to Jesus and run to Him for refuge? Whenever you are having a hard day with a squeamish stomach or a sad psyche or aching arms, run for shelter to your Savior and feel His loving presence anew. "Be good to me, God—and now! I've run to you for dear life. I'm hiding out under your wings until the hurricane blows over. I call out to High God, the God who holds me together" (Ps. 57:1-2).

"How exquisite your love, O God! How eager we are to run under your wings, to eat our fill at the banquet you spread as you fill our tankards with Eden spring water. You're a fountain of cascading light, and you open our eyes to light" (Ps. 36:7-8).

I call to you, God, because I'm sure of an answer. So—answer! Bend your ear! Listen sharp! Paint grace-graffiti on the fences; take in your frightened children who are running from the neighborhood bullies straight to you. Keep your eye on me; hide me under your cool wing feathers from the wicked who are out to get me, from mortal enemies closing in.

—Psalms 17:6-9

He who dwells in the secret place of the Most High shall remain stable *and* fixed under the shadow of the Almighty [whose power no foe can withstand]. I will say of the Lord, He is my Refuge and my Fortress, My God; on Him I lean *and* rely, *and* in Him I (confidently) trust! [Then] He will cover you with His pinions, and under His wings shall you trust *and* find refuge; His truth *and* His faithfulness are a shield and a buckler.

—Psalms 91:1-2, 4 AB

# A GLIMMER OF HIS HEART

*T*HE STATEMENT STOPPED me in my tracks: "Now you know how I felt."

Let me catch you up on the week this happened, which had been a blur of activity. My dear friend's mother was battling cancer, and they had just moved her into their home. Trying to help care for this classy southern lady was an absolute joy, for any small kindness was greeted with such gratitude. Her sweet spirit made the events of that day even more difficult to swallow, though. A nurse's aide had come to administer her shower, or should I say, watch her take her shower. But she gave no steadying hand, nor did she show any concern for her safety, and not surprisingly, the dear lady fell—hard—and she couldn't get up. The insult to her dignity was bad enough, but the blatant lack of remorse was what had me so fired up in my lament to God.

And that's when He said it, "Now you know how I felt." Oh, my. The impact of those words took my breath away. I had just experienced a glimmer of the Father's fury at the reproach to His Son, beginning in a garden called Gethsemane. The unrelenting pain and the unrepentant hearts. Did they not know Who He was?

But my heavenly Father and I reacted very differently to the injustices we saw. I proclaimed loudly that it would never happen again. God just watched as the cruelty and horror against His Son escalated to the point of death. And then, totally out of my realm of understanding,

He forgave those who perpetrated the crime, which, down through the ages, included me! It was a taste of what my God chose to allow that Good Friday. He permitted the pain because of His love for us. I gained a new understanding of His love that day, for it was deeper than I had ever imagined. I also felt a more profound gratitude for what Calvary cost the Father as He watched, for it was higher than I could ever comprehend.

Have you ever really thought about what Jesus the Son and God the Father endured for each one of us because of their amazing love for us? Contemplate it right now, with a renewed sense of awe.

If you have never accepted the gift of eternal life that Jesus bought for you that day, then today is the day to receive His perfect once-for-all payment for all that you have ever done wrong or ever will do. Don't delay. He is waiting for you. Just pray this simple prayer:

Dear God,

Dress me in Your righteousness right now. Remove my sin-stained clothes and fit me perfectly with the salvation shoes that Jesus bought for me on the cross. Lead me on the path You have planned for me. I trust You to give me whatever shoes I need because You know the roads I will take. Thank You for Your great love for me. Amen

_____

(Insert your name and date)

He was beaten, he was tortured, but he didn't say a word. Like a lamb taken to be slaughtered and like a sheep being sheared, he took it all in silence. Still, it's what God had in mind all along, to crush him with pain. The plan was that he give himself as an offering for sin so that he'd see life come from it—life, life, and more life.

—Isaiah 53:7, 10

This is how much God loved the world. He gave his Son, his one and only Son. And this is why: so that no one need be destroyed; by believing in him, anyone can have a whole and lasting life. God didn't go to all that trouble of sending his Son merely to point an accusing finger, telling the world how bad it was. He came to help, to put the world right again.

—John 3:16, 17

The Father loves the Son extravagantly. He turned everything over to him so he could give it away—a lavish distribution of gifts. That is why whoever accepts and trusts the Son gets in on everything, life complete and forever!

—John 3:34, 35

My purpose in writing is simply this: that you who believe in God's Son will know beyond the shadow of a doubt that you have eternal life, the reality and not the illusion. And how bold and free we then become in his presence, freely asking according to his will, sure that he's listening.

—1 John 5:13, 14

# FEET WASHING

*I*T WAS PROBABLY a phone call, or possibly a letter, that informed you of your breast cancer. Either way, you were changed forever. Life is suddenly reduced to the bare necessities when you deal with cancer of any kind. Coming face to face with a life-threatening illness forces all of us to deal with our own mortality and our own consciences.

Because of that, God gives us the opportunity to have conversations that would have been too frightening to attempt before our cancer diagnosis. He has opened wide the door for talks with those we love, or even with those estranged from us. The possibility and promise of forgiveness has suddenly become our companion on this road—a friend previously ignored, perhaps, on our life walk.

As this new avenue of forgiveness presented itself to me, I began to take stock of my relationships and found that some of them needed mending. I needed to ask forgiveness from some friends and to extend it to others. I didn't have the time or desire to disobey God on this any longer. I wanted my conscience clean and my broken relationships restored.

Here's my story of how God blessed one "forgiveness conversation" as I talked it over with Him. *She reminded me of You today, Lord. I asked for her forgiveness, and her response resembled Yours. I hadn't wanted to confess, but it was Holy Week, and I knew that my Easter would be less than a Hallelujah day if I ignored Your stirrings in my heart. You longed for me to be free of this burden, held way too long. I had confessed my sin repeatedly to You but had never admitted it to my wronged friend. I had swept my bad behavior under the rug and thought the dust would never reappear. But the room of our friendship bore the aroma of uncleanliness, and no sachet would disguise it. A full admission of my wrongdoing and a heartfelt apology were necessary for me to feel clean again. The balm of my friend's forgiveness was needed to freshen the air.*

*But repentance is not easy. It requires You to reveal the hurt and broken places in our lives. Thanks be to God, though, for Your help to do that! I explained to her the pain in my heart that led to the sin and tearfully asked for her pardon. The tender look on her face told me that she understood. Just like You. She showed Your heart. She didn't say how left out I had made her feel; she just forgave me. And suddenly, all the twinges of guilt that had edged our days together were gone. The joy of our friendship was renewed, even enhanced. And I was set free to receive all the blessings You had been waiting to pour out to me.*

*Maundy Thursday was a glorious night. As I went forward to get my feet washed, I felt Your anointing for what You had been calling me to do. Now I could do it in freedom. And it all began with my friend reminding me of You. Help me to resemble You today, Lord. Make me as quick to forgive as she was. She reminded me of You.*

Will you ask God, right now, to take off your prissy shoes, and put on His forgiveness shoes? If so, prayerfully ask Him to show you the people in your life who are in need of your forgiveness or from whom you need to seek pardon. Cancer is not the only thing in each of our lives that needs healing. Receive God's abundant healing.

These verses will help you:

"GOD, GOD, a God of mercy and grace, endlessly patient—so much love, so deeply true—loyal in love for a thousand generations, forgiving iniquity, rebellion, and sin" (Ex. 34:6).

"You're well-known as good and forgiving, big hearted to all who ask for help" (Ps. 86:5).

"Be gentle with one another, sensitive. Forgive one another as quickly and thoroughly as God in Christ forgave you" (Eph. 4:32).

Watch what God does, and then you do it, like children who learn proper behavior from their parents. Mostly what God does is love you. Keep company with him and learn a life of love. Observe how Christ loved us. His love was not cautious but extravagant. He didn't love in order to get something from us but to give everything of himself to us. Love like that.

—Ephesians 5:1-2

So, chosen by God for this new life of love, dress in the wardrobe God picked out for you: compassion, kindness, humility, quiet strength, discipline. Be even-tempered, content with second place, quick to forgive an offense. Forgive as quickly and completely as the Master forgave you. And regardless of what else you put on, wear love. It's your basic, all-purpose garment. Never be without it.

—Colossians 3:12-14

# CRADLED IN HIS ARMS

$S$OMETHING ABOUT HIS face resembled that of his father. Maybe the way his lips formed that timid smile, or possibly his longing, winsome eyes. Something about him brought David's heart back to Jonathan. How could he not love Mephibosheth? Do you know his story? It is a wonderful little treasure in 2 Samuel. Let me paraphrase it for you. David and Jonathan, King Saul's son, are covenant friends. They have vowed to show kindness to each other and their families forever. But Jonathan and his father, King Saul, are both killed on the same day, and David mourns. Later, David asks if anyone of King Saul's household still lives, so that he might show the person kindness for Jonathan's sake.

It turns out that Jonathan has a son named Mephibosheth. After the news of Saul and Jonathan's deaths, the nurse fleeing with young Mephibosheth dropped him. He was lame from that day on. Now it was routine in the ancient Middle East for kings to kill the children of former rulers. So consider Mephibosheth's alarm when he was summoned by King David! But David remembered his covenant with Jonathan and wanted to show kindness to his son by welcoming him to his table. Mephibosheth was overwhelmed. To be carried to the king's table and allowed to eat there for the rest of his life was incomprehensible.

Could he have realized that God was using him as a lesson in grace? Do we understand that our lives are just like this? We, too, were wounded by the fall, in the garden of Eden. Just like Mephibosheth, we were lost and forsaken until the king summoned us to His table. We don't belong there any more than Mephibosheth did. But every time God looks at us, He too, sees His Son, and He loves us because of that resemblance.

We are all crippled in some way, like Jonathan's son. Breast cancer has attacked our bodies and we feel broken. We are like shorn lambs that need to be held close to the Shepherd's heart. We are the bruised reeds He promised not to break. We are broken in body, but even more, our spirits can get crushed as we walk this hard road.

We may have abandoned our prissy shoes for sensible ones, but maybe we need more than different shoes; maybe we need His tender healing touch for our skinned and bleeding feet. Jesus came to bind us wherever we are broken and He carries us to His table because of His great love for us.

Mephibosheth's story is our story, too. Remember that the next time you come for communion. Jesus carries us to His table just as we are and brings His saving grace to us as we take of the bread and the wine. Ask God to show you His heart for you the next time you come to His table.

"It so happened that Saul's son Jonathan, had a son who was maimed in both feet. When he was five years old, the report on Saul and Jonathan came from Jezreel. His nurse picked him up and ran, but in her hurry to get away she fell and the boy was maimed. His name was Mephibosheth" (2 Sam. 4:4).

"And Mephibosheth ate at David's table, just like one of the royal family" (2 Sam. 9:11).

"Energize the limp hands, strengthen the rubbery knees. Tell fearful souls, 'Courage! Take heart! God is here, right here, on his way to put things right and redress all wrongs. He's on his way! He'll save you'" (Isa. 35:3-4).

"Like a shepherd, he will care for his flock, gathering the lambs in his arms, hugging them as he carries them" (Isa. 40:11).

"So he became their Savor. In all their troubles, he was troubled, too. He didn't send someone else to help them. He did it himself, in person. Out of his own love and pity he redeemed them. He rescued them and carried them along for a long, long time" (Isa. 63:8-9).

"I'll make a covenant with them that will last forever, a covenant to stick with them no matter what, and work for their good" (Jer. 32:40).

"Immense in mercy and with an incredible love, he embraced us. He took our sin-dead lives and made us alive in Christ. He did all this on his own, with no help from us! Then he picked us up and set us down in highest heaven in company with Jesus, our Messiah" (Eph. 2:4-6).

# WEIGHTLIFTERS WITH
# WEIGHTY WORDS

*I* AM A member of this sisterhood none of us chose. God has positioned us on a hilltop where we are more visible than normal and more easily heard. We've talked about forgiveness for ourselves (Tended) and forgiveness for others (Feet Washing), but what about *eternal* forgiveness? Maybe, through our breast cancer diagnosis, God has given us a new boldness to present Jesus as the answer to someone's problems now that we have experienced Him as the divine solution.

God's heart has always been about relationships, and He longs to touch others through our walk. But will we let Him? Will we obediently follow where He leads us, knowing that He longs to give "a word in season to him who is weary" (Isaiah 50:4 NKJV)?

Through our breast cancer, God has opened doors for us to speak to others of His eternal forgiveness. That alone could be the divine blueprint for the path we have been called to walk. But will we take off our prissy shoes and willingly put on His salvation shoes on another's behalf?

Years ago, my heart was profoundly touched by a speaker at my children's school. It is my prayer that these words will also open your eyes to God's heart for those who don't yet know Him. Hear, with God's heart.

His T-shirt, which could not hide his bulging biceps or taut physique, simply read, "Eternity is too long to be wrong." He was a Christian strength trainer whom I had invited to speak at my children's school.

The students sat captivated as he wrapped a half-inch thick straight steel bar into an oval around a thin fourth-grade girl. He spoke of his relationship with Jesus, but I honestly don't remember his message. I will never forget the words on his shirt, however.

Those seven words gave a new intensity to my prayers for unsaved loved ones and acquaintances. It was bad enough to imagine them without Jesus at the moment of their deaths. But to contemplate their unrelenting, infinite time in hell was nearly unbearable. Thus began my "salvation prayer list." What once had only existed in my heart was now a tangible written roll call, which continues to grow.

Eternity is a long time, and some of the people we know and love will "get it wrong." I have a dear relative who, unless something changes in his life, will get eternity wrong. Only God knows all the tears I have shed over that dreadful possibility. As a new Christian at eleven years of age, I pled with God for his salvation, and even offered to die myself if he would just "get it" at my funeral.

Finally, my tender Lord assured me that He had already died for him, and I did not need to "add on" to Calvary. Over the years, I have had many heartfelt conversations with this relative, to no avail. The Lord has convinced me through a wonderful friend named Marie to just love him and pray for him, which I continue to do.

I am sure that each of you has dearly beloved family members and friends in this predicament. These prayers of ours, on their behalf, could have eternal payoffs, and no prayers are dearer to God's heart than these.

Remember the thief on the cross whose first-ever prayer was answered without a moment's hesitation? Jesus is passionate about the salvation of those for whom He died. It is high time that we were, too. So before you close this devotional and get caught up in the busyness of the day, ask God to open your eyes to those around you who are in desperate need of His salvation. Ask Him to give you the courage to lovingly start a dialogue with them about forever matters. Because eternity *is* too long to be wrong.

These passages underscore God's desire for all to come to Him:

"Tell them, as sure as I am the living God, I take no pleasure from the death of the wicked. I want the wicked to change their ways and live.

Turn your life around! Reverse your evil ways! Why *die*, [insert person's name]?" (Ezek. 33:11)

"My dear friends, if you know people who have wandered off from God's truth, don't write them off. Go after them. Get them back and you will have rescued precious lives from destruction and prevented an epidemic of wandering away from God" (James 5:19-20).

"He wants not only us but *everyone* saved, you know, everyone to get to know the truth *we've* learned: that there's one God and only one, and one Priest-Mediator between God and us—Jesus, who offered himself in exchange for everyone held captive by sin, to set them all free" (1 Tim. 2:3-6).

Don't overlook the obvious here, friends. With God, one day is as good as a thousand years, a thousand years as a day. God isn't late with his promise as some measure lateness. He is restraining himself on account of you, holding back the End because he doesn't want anyone lost. He's giving everyone space and time to change. But when the Day of God's Judgement does come, it will be unannounced, like a thief. The sky will collapse with a thunderous bang, everything disintegrating in a huge conflagration, earth and all its works exposed to the scrutiny of Judgement.

—2 Peter 3:8-10

"This is the testimony in essence: God gave us eternal life; the life is in his Son. So, whoever has the Son, has life; whoever rejects the Son, rejects life" (1 John 5:11-12).

# A STONE NAMED EBENEZER

*I*T WAS A perfectly smooth, oval stone, and it bore just one word, lovingly written in Sharpie: *COURAGE*. It had been left at my front door shortly after my breast cancer diagnosis by a dear friend named Carolyn who taught a Bible study with me. It sits on my kitchen sink to remind me of the vital biblical lesson it portrays.

Do you know about stones in the Old Testament? They were all over the landscape of the Middle East, and they were used in many different ways. Sometimes they were the building materials for homes and walls. Other times they formed altars. But still other times they were used as a marker or memorial of a significant event where God intervened in the lives of His people.

In Genesis 49:24 (NKJV), God is called "the Stone of Israel." After the crossing of the Red Sea and the parting of the Jordan River, stones were set up as memorials to God's faithfulness and deliverance. After He miraculously saved the Israelites from the Philistines, Samuel, the prophet, names his stone, "Ebenezer," meaning "Stone of Help" because "Heretofore the Lord has helped us."

It has been said that "Life is like the Hebrew language. You can only understand it if you read it backwards." Reading your life backwards can illuminate blessings you would not normally recognize because you clearly see that God *has* helped you up until now. What fears have you had in your pink journey that have not come true? What difficulties

71

have been surmounted? One year, to the day, after my breast cancer diagnosis, I wrote these words in my journal:

"My mind is taken back, over and over, to the upcoming events of last year at this time, and the first days of my knowledge of my breast cancer. You have deepened my understanding of Your faithfulness and made richer my friendships. You have used this journey to make me more confident and more authentic. You have shown me the bounty of this wonderful area where You have placed me—its people are generous and compassionate. And You have given me a glimpse of the power of prayer—how it knits together the broken places not only in our bodies, but in our emotions, our relationships and our souls. This breast cancer journey has been by Your Hand, an unexpected blessing in many ways."

My mother has dementia. It is a heartbreaking disease. She has forgotten people and events once very important to her. They no longer bring her joy or solace or strength. Down the road, I have no control over dementia or my cognitive ability or memory, but right now, I do determine what is placed in my heart's mind. I want to be ever mindful of the spiritual events God has etched upon the tablet of my heart. To no longer marvel at those experiences where God clearly revealed Himself to me would be appalling. Those occasions where God paraded His power in my life must not be allowed to slip from my memory.

In this fast-paced, toss-it-away world we live in, it takes a deliberate exercise of our will to accomplish this, but the cost of not succeeding is enormous. If breast cancer is the journey we are on, then thankfulness is the road home. So remember my stone. Make one of your own if it will help you. Write on it whatever word God places on your heart. Then ask God to give you the courage to praise Him as you walk your pink journey.

"But the Master, GOD, has something to say to this: 'Watch closely. I'm laying a foundation in Zion, a solid, granite foundation, squared and true. And this is the meaning of the stone: A TRUSTING LIFE WON'T TOPPLE'" (Isa. 28:16).

Lord Jesus, give each of us the courage to always find reasons to praise You. Help us to look back with hearts of gratitude for what You have done for us in the past; to look around with eyes open to see Your touch in our lives today; and to look up to You in adoration for what You do for us, but even more, for Who You are for us—our Rock! Amen.

"Only take heed, and guard your life diligently, lest you forget the things which your eyes have seen and lest they depart from your [mind and] heart all the days of your life" (Deut. 4:9 AB).

> When all the nation had fully passed over the Jordan, the Lord said to Joshua, take twelve men from among the people, one man out of every tribe, and command them, take twelve stones out of the midst of the Jordan from the place where the priests' feet stood firm; carry them over with you and leave them at the place where you lodge tonight. And the people came up out of the Jordan...And those twelve stones which they took out of the Jordan Joshua set up in Gilgal. And he said to the Israelites, When your children ask their fathers in time to come, what do these stones mean? You shall let your children know, Israel came over this Jordan on dry ground. For the Lord your God dried up the waters of the Jordan for you until you passed over, as the Lord your God did to the Red Sea, which He dried up for us until we passed over, that all the peoples of the earth may know that the hand of the Lord is mighty and that you may reverence *and* fear the Lord your God forever.
>
> —Joshua 4:1-3, 19-24 AB

"Then Samuel took a stone...and he called the name of it Ebenezer [stone of help], saying, Heretofore the Lord has helped us" (1 Sam. 7:12 AB).

# SURCEE

*H*AVING BEEN RAISED by southern parents and then transplanted to the South over two decades ago, I have long understood what a "surcee" was. Imagine my surprise when I could find no mention of this delightful word in the dictionary. Finally, I located a reference to it through an American regional entry. A surcee is a small gift or favor, often given as a surprise. It is a gift for no reason. The term, used mainly in the South, may have come from the Irish or Scottish verb, *sussie,* or the French verb, *souci,* both meaning "to care" or "to trouble oneself."

I prefer to think that the origin is ultimately heavenly, and I'll tell you why. Not twenty-four hours after I had been contemplating the joys of such unexpected gifts, God gave me a perfect example of one. While grocery shopping the next morning, I was greeted by the produce salesperson with this welcome, "Make sure you look on the table by the flowers. There are free roses there." A true flower freak, I dashed in that direction, secretly expecting to find flowers long past their prime with either few or dried-up petals. Imagine my glee when I glimpsed not a few but a dozen long-stemmed roses whose petals were not only beautiful and velvety soft, but the richest, most royal shade of crimson. These roses would have been appreciated regardless of their color, but they were blood-red by design.

The Giver of all things was teaching me an object lesson, and the redemptive color was deliberately detailed for a heavenly purpose. I sensed that these blooms were divinely intended for a specific friend of mine, as a token of love for a beloved child from her adoring Father. The abundance of joy on my friend's face on receiving this unexpected gift confirmed my impression.

God loves to give surcees. It is His character and His delight to send heavenly gifts "for no reason" to His children. The question is, do we even notice or acknowledge them? What joys we miss when our eyes are not attentive to unexpected little gifts from God! Ask Him today for the openness to not only perceive them, but also receive them with a grateful heart. They're sent to make your day!

Just before this book went to print, the scenario with the flowers repeated itself. But this time, the red roses were for the young-at-heart lady mentioned in "A Glimmer of His Heart," who was very quickly approaching her wedding feast with the Lamb. They were a "can't wait to see you" bouquet from the most thoughtful Bridegroom to His beloved bride.

Ask God to open your eyes to all the little surcees He showers on you daily. They will bring a new lift to your weary footsteps.

"What a stack of blessings you have piled up for those who worship you" (Ps. 31:19).

"Many, O Lord my God, are the wonderful works which You have done, and Your thoughts toward us; no one can compare with You! If I should declare and speak of them, they are too many to be numbered" (Ps. 40:5 AB).

"No doubt about it! God is good—good to good people, good to the good-hearted. But I nearly missed it, missed seeing his goodness" (Ps. 73:1-2).

"Open your mouth wide and I will fill it" (Ps. 81:10 AB).

"If you then, evil as you are, know how to give good *and* advantageous gifts to your children, how much more will your Father Who is in heaven [perfect as He is] give good *and* advantageous things to those who keep on asking Him!" (Matt. 7:11 AB)

"I'll make a list of GOD's gracious dealings, all the things GOD has done that need praising, all the generous bounties of GOD, his great goodness to the family of [insert your name]. Compassion lavished, love extravagant" (Isa. 63:7).

# EVERY LEANIN' SIDE

*I*T IS MY favorite summer necklace, this triple-stranded pink beaded choker that I wear so often. Ecclesiastes 4:12 says that "a threefold cord is not quickly broken" (NKJV). As we walk this pink journey, we all need to have a threefold cord undergirding us. That triple strand is composed of God's Word, God's praise, and God's people. God's Word is our fundamental underpinning. It is our authority, our support, our truth. Hebrews 4:12-13 says, "God means what he says. What he says goes. His powerful Word is sharp as a surgeon's scalpel, cutting through everything, whether doubt or defense, laying us open to listen and obey. Nothing and no one is impervious to God's Word. We can't get away from it—no matter what."

Scripture is our primary lifeline, but it is reinforced by two other cords. One of those is God's praise. Psalm 146:1-2 says, "Hallelujah! O my soul, praise GOD! All my life long I'll praise GOD, singing songs to my God as long as I live." Our bodies may be sick with cancer right now, but our hearts are healthy if they can always praise God for something. No matter how bad we feel, or how dire our prognosis, our God is always worthy of our glory.

The last strand of our strong cord is God's people. The very first thing I did after my diagnosis was assemble my support team. You can't walk this journey alone, and God certainly doesn't mean for you to. Remember to pray for these friends who are lifting you up, though. The week after my diagnosis, I realized how much they needed my prayers. I was listening to my phone messages and wrote this in my journal, "I was struck by the fact that my friends were having a harder time with this than I was! Their prayers were giving me peace and lifting the burden off of my shoulders and placing it on all of their shoulders. Lord, teach them to give those burdens to You. Take the pain and fear from their hearts and voices."

As often as you can, worship God with your team. Lifting up praise and intercessions as the body of Christ raises our hearts and minds to the place where God wants us. Scripture says that God inhabits the praises of His people. Before my chemotherapy, I was nervous about how it would make me feel. At church, I was able to lay those fears and concerns at the cross. I wrote, "It is always so wonderful to worship at All Saints. My fears from yesterday just melted away, as I worshipped my wonderful, loving heavenly Father. I laid down my own strength to be strong and upbeat and cheerful and asked for heavenly strength to do all of these things."

I have a very special friend named Susan. Watching her life has taught me much about trusting my Lord for everything. Her prayers over me have been a special gift because she is so honest and humble in her requests to God. She prayed for Him to support me "on every leanin' side." Isn't that just what we need? Some days we lean in one direction and other days, we're thrown in a different way. Lord, support us on every leanin' side!

Where are you leaning today? Let the Word and praise and your wonderful intercessors support you. Let them know your needs and your anxieties and then feel your loving Father's support, through them.

I can think of two stories that speak to this support God wants us to have from His people. The first one is in Exodus 17. The Israelites are fighting the Amalekites, and Moses is praying for their victory. As long as his arms are raised in intercession, the Israelites win. But eventually his arms get tired, and the battle goes to Amalek. Two friends sit him on a stone and hold up his hands, one on either side, so that Amalek is defeated. Your support teams are your arm raisers, interceding for you and supporting you on every leaning side.

In the New Testament, four friends bring a sick man to Jesus for healing. But the crowd is so great that they can't get close to Him. So they climb up to the roof, remove the tiles, and lower him down on his mat, right in front of Jesus. This is a visual picture of your support team—they are your stretcher-bearers.

One especially hard week, I sent this e-mail to my support team: "It seems like a very long time since I've written you, but this one will be short because I am very low on energy. Y'all have become my stretcher-bearers this week, for I have no strength of my own. I'm so thankful that I have a very comfy bed, because it has become my dwelling place. My chemo last Friday and Neulasta shot this past Monday have totally drained me. I'm like poor old Moses in Exodus 17, who can't lift up his arms anymore, so Aaron and Hur lift them up, and the battle is won. Keep lifting me up in prayer, so that we can win the battle, too."

I wrote in my journal that "this breast cancer journey has taught me invaluable lessons about the depths of fatigue, when you just can't do anything and you don't really even care. The value of stretcher-bearers will forever be etched on my memory." The day after I came home from the hospital following my second mastectomy and reconstructive surgery, I journalled this: "Lord, You are so merciful. Yesterday in the hospital I was reading Philippians 4, where Paul talks about lacking nothing. This morning as I took my first shower with four drains to deal with (I finally just threw them over my shoulder!), I got sad for a moment, thinking how nice it would have been to have my Momma here to pamper and help me. But the situation instead is that she doesn't even understand anything that has happened to me in the last year because of her dementia. Then I focused on what I have—more mothers and sisters, brothers and fathers in Christ than I could ever imagine, and the tears stopped, and I realized that I was humming the children's song, 'Count your blessings, name them one by one, count your blessings, see what God has done.' Thank You once again that I can say that I lack nothing."

Your stretcher-bearers are a gift to you from your caring Savior, Who wants to support you on every leaning side. They will hold up your arms, keep your feet steady, and when you need it, even carry you, by the grace of God. He is your Great Supporter. Receive all that He offers you in this triple-stranded cord.

Are any of your strands missing? Prayerfully ask God to help you make sure you are lifted up by His Word, His praise, and His people. "Bear one another's burdens, and so fulfill the law of Christ" (Gal. 6:2 NKJV).

Joshua did what Moses ordered in order to fight Amalek. And Moses, Aaron, and Hur went to the top of the hill. It turned out that whenever Moses raised his hands, Israel was winning, but whenever he lowered his hands, Amalek was winning. But Moses' hands got tired. So they got a stone and set it under him. He sat on it and Aaron and Hur held up his hands, one on each side. So his hands remained steady until the sun went down. Joshua defeated Amalek and its army in battle.

—Exodus 17:10-13

Some men arrived carrying a paraplegic on a stretcher. They were looking for a way to get into the house and set him before Jesus. When they couldn't find a way in because of the crowd, they went up on the roof, removed some tiles, and let him down in the middle of everyone, right in front of Jesus.

—Luke 5:18-20

# STOMPIN' ON
# SNAKES

*I* HAD SEEN His infinite power in my life time and time again, but never in such a dramatic display as this demonstration that literally had me shaking in my boots. On Saturday morning, I went for my regular walk, which takes nearly an hour if I walk at a brisk pace. I use this time to exercise but also to worship God in His creation and listen to His voice as I am quiet before Him. Shortly after I started my walk, a verse came to my mind. Now that is not unusual, but the verse that filled my thoughts that morning was not one you generally dwell on.

It was Genesis 3:15, "He shall bruise your head, and you shall bruise His heel" (NKJV). This is part of the redemptive covenant, and it is the Lord speaking to the serpent in the garden of Eden after the fall. Jesus would be hurt by a blow to His heel, but Satan would be crushed with a blow to his head. It is not your run-of-the-mill verse that comes into your mind. I thought how strange that was, but I then dismissed it and kept on walking.

As I finished my course and was nearly back to my home, the reason for that particular verse became amazingly clear. Not two feet in front of me was a baby copperhead snake, crawling right across my path. Now when I say "tiny," I'm talking about a really small snake—only six inches long. But it had the familiar markings and the triangular head, and I knew that this little baby snake had venom, too.

If you haven't gathered yet from this book, I'll just tell you—I am a girly-girl, which makes what I am going to tell you even more remarkable. With Genesis 3:15 resounding in my head, I stomped on that snake's head. It, of course, convulsed all over the place, which freaked me out, but I kept stomping on it to make sure it was dead because I didn't want to have to deal with it later when it grew up! I caught my breath, gathered my composure, and started walking again, now just a few houses from my home, when right in front of my path wiggled another copperhead, only this one was fatter and a foot long. By this time, I realized that this was not just a coincidence. God had purposely brought that verse to my mind and now He was giving me the reason. I hoped this was the last example! My reaction time was slower with this second larger snake, but with great fear and trembling and a quick, "Help me, Lord!" I once again lifted up my foot and crashed it down on the snake's head. My heart was beating a mile a minute as I repeatedly stepped on this squirming, angry serpent. I nearly sprinted home, breathless with excitement and awe at what had just happened.

This snake encounter filled my every thought but left me speechless. My only response was to stammer heavenward, "What was *that* all about, Lord?" Then a quiet understanding began to fill my heart and mind. It was as if God was speaking these words to me: "Satan, like snakes, is real, and his venom is poisonous. But I, Yahweh, am infinitely larger and stronger, and I have already defeated him. I continue to step on his head, just as I have always done."

The Lord showed me two principles that morning. The first was proportion. We give Satan way too much power in our minds. God stomps on him as easily as I did that six-inch snake. The second principle was priority. Yes, Satan is small in proportion to God, but dealing with him when he first rears his ugly head needs to be a priority, because his influences and intimidation grow, if left unchecked—like the twelve-inch snake. The longer we allow his presence in our lives, the harder he is to step on. Whew! I got it, God. (I was afraid to look up any Biblical references to cobras or lions—I didn't want to play show-and-tell anymore!) I'll never forget that live illustration that day. Satan had lost his power to intimidate me. Now, when he tries to spook me with his big, bad talk, I just envision that skinny six-inch snake writhing in pain as it succumbed to my sneakers. And speaking of sneakers, did you know that the Greek word for "victory" or "victorious" is spelled n-i-k-e, and the word for "overcomer" is very similar. (These words are used in the 1 John verses at the end of this devotion.)

Believe it or not, God had one more point He wanted to make that weekend. The next morning my son, Carey, said he almost woke me up at midnight when he read his daily devotion, for this was the verse: "Behold! I have given you authority *and* power to trample upon serpents and scorpions, and [physical and mental strength and ability] over all the power that the enemy [possesses]; and nothing shall in any way harm you" (Luke 10:19 AB). He wanted to make sure I didn't miss any of His points, and I didn't.

What about you? Are there any places in your life where you have let Satan seem way too big and God seem way too small? If that is true, confess it now, and receive your stompin' on snakes, overcoming, victorious shoes from your bigger-than-you-can-ever-imagine God! These verses will help you:

"You are of God, little children, and have overcome them, because He who is in you is greater than he who is in the world" (1 John 4:4 NKJV).

"For whatever is born of God overcomes the world. And this is the victory that has overcome the world—our faith. Who is he who overcomes the world, but he who believes that Jesus is the Son of God?" (1 John 5:4-5 NKJV).

GOD is my strength, GOD is my song, and yes! GOD is my salvation. *This* is the kind of God I have and I'm telling the world! *This* is the God of my father—I'm spreading the news far and wide! GOD is a fighter, pure GOD, through and through. Your strong right hand, GOD, shimmers with power; your strong right hand shatters the enemy. In your mighty majesty you smash your upstart enemies. Who compares with you among gods, O GOD? Who compares with you in power, in holy majesty, in awesome praises, wonder-working God? Let GOD rule forever, for eternity!

—Exodus 15:1-3, 6, 11, 18

# AUTHOR *AND* FINISHER

$S$ATAN HAD TRIED to use tormenting lies and insinuations to raise havoc in my soul. I knew that it was time to stand firm on the Truth. The father of all lies had droned on and on about the possibility, even the probability, of my cancer returning, and I had heard enough.

I went to the heavenly throne room with my basket-load of Satan-inspired fears. I laid them on the mercy seat where the One Who numbers my days ever intercedes for me, and I made this request, "Lord, grant that my dying, whenever and however it occurs, will be a means of glorifying You and drawing others into a closer relationship with You. In Your mercy, give a glimpse of Your eternal splendor to those around me, and let it confirm their faith in all things heavenly. Amen."

Then the most miraculous thing happened! Peace flooded my soul—peace that was not dependent on my understanding of what might happen one day. For the Shepherd of my soul set up watch over this needy little lamb of His, and He has kept Satan's wolves at bay ever since. Satan no longer harasses me about the details of my death, and since that day, rather than fearing death, I look forward to using my final breaths to draw others to my precious Lord.

Jesus took the dread away and replaced it with expectation, and I am sincerely grateful. As the Alpha and the Omega, the Beginning and the End, the Author and Finisher of our faith, He is trustworthy to carry us from this world into the next. I know neither when nor how

He plans to take me to heaven, but if I can trust Him with the location of my eternity, I can trust Him with the means of getting me there. The Lord began my faith on that day when my heart really saw Him for the first time. He will finish my faith when my eyes see Him forever, and it will be in the best way, and at the best time—a route ordained by our omniscient, loving Father. Hallelujah!

What about you? Death is always a possibility when you are dealing with cancer, but fearing death does not have to be part of it. Go to the One Who knows you, loves you, and has the perfect plan to take you home to be with Him, and ask Him to remove any fear that Satan has placed in your heart. His perfect love will cast out all fear.

Here are some verses that help me in this area:

"Now you've got my feet on the life path, all radiant from the shining of your face. Ever since you took my hand, I'm on the right way" (Ps. 16:11).

"And me? I plan on looking you full in the face. When I get up, I'll see your full stature and live heaven on earth" (Ps. 17:15).

"Precious (important and no light matter) in the sight of the Lord is the death of His saints (His loving ones)" (Ps. 116:15 AB).

Keep your eyes on *Jesus*, who both began and finished this race we're in. Study how he did it. Because he never lost sight of where he was headed—that exhilarating finish in and with God —he could put up with anything along the way: cross, shame, whatever. And now he's *there*, in the place of honor, right alongside God. When you find yourselves flagging in your faith, go over that story again, item by item, that long litany of hostility he plowed through. *That* will shoot adrenaline into your souls!

—Hebrews 12:2-3

# HOPE FLOATS

*I*T WAS A God-ordained reunion with our cherished friends (my husband and I met at their wedding!) I had been having terrible side effects from a new drug prescribed for me, and they felt led to come from Atlanta to pray for me and seek God's face together. The joy of that precious fellowship was sweet, but I believe God's primary purpose for that trip was a two-word statement that Katie said to me, totally unaware of its impact.

"Hope floats" was the divine message spoken through her lips. The eternal truth of those words resounded in my heart and made a home there—a comforting, inviting home where I wanted to dwell. I longed to curl up in the essence of that promise and wrap it luxuriously around me forever. Hope—it is God's amazing gift for this trip we are all on—traveling with us to energize us and draw us close to the One Who planned this path.

As human beings, we live and move inside time and space. Hope is the gift that beckons us to soar with the Spirit of God because it bridges time. It is our glimpse of glory. Without hope, there is no light at the end of the tunnel, only dark despair or, at best, timeworn, ongoing sameness. But hope sings out the change—that God has intersected our world and our lives and has given us a new path and a new destination. This present that God offers us must be accepted, for hope, like its Father, is a gentleman and will not intrude where it is not invited.

Let's welcome this fellow traveler on our journey; let's embrace this expectantly waiting one because hope transcends time. It rides from the present to the past to the future. It is never just for a moment.

My grandmother knew this truth. She died of breast cancer at twenty-eight, leaving an eight-year-old son. She lived above her circumstances though, because of hope. She knew that stars which dimly shine at dusk dazzle the eyes in the deepest night. She understood that the steeper the path for the day, the tighter you need to grasp the Father's hand, in hope. Her husband and son were both named for the famous preacher, Charles Haddon Spurgeon, whose writings have left an indelible mark on my life. Maybe my grandmother knew my favorite quote of his, for she certainly demonstrated it in her short life. "Our griefs cannot mar the melody of our praise; we reckon them to be the bass part of our life's song, 'To God be the glory!'"[4]

It is my prayer that I, too, will allow God's eternal hope to fill my heart and raise me above my circumstances. Today, are you bogged down with chemotherapy or radiation? Are you struggling with those horrid drains for one more week? Maybe just the everyday stresses of life on top of the angst of doctor's appointments or waiting for results has your heart as low as your white blood count. If this sounds like where you are, ask God to lift you above the details of your life through His Word, as you read these verses. Let Him fit your feet with the hopeful shoes you will need to walk through this day.

"I'm on a diet of tears—tears for breakfast, tears for supper. All day long people knock at my door, pestering, 'Where is this God of yours?' Why are you down in the dumps, dear soul? Why are you crying the blues? Fix my eyes on God—soon I'll be praising again. He puts a smile on my face. He's my God" (Ps. 42:3, 5).

"So, let's *do* it—full of belief, confident that we're presentable inside and out. Let's keep a firm grip on the promises that keep us going. He always keeps his word" (Heb. 10:22-23).

"So, we're not giving up. How could we! Even though on the outside it often looks like things are falling apart on us, on the inside, where God is making new life, not a day goes by without his unfolding grace" (2 Cor. 4:16).

There's more to come: We continue to shout our praise even when we're hemmed in with troubles; because we know how troubles can develop passionate patience in us, and how that patience in turn forges the tempered steel of virtue, keeping us alert for whatever God will do next. In alert expectancy such as this, we're never left feeling shortchanged. Quite the contrary—we can't round up enough containers to hold everything God generously pours into our lives through the Holy Spirit!

—Romans 5:3-5

So friends, take a firm stand, feet on the ground and head high. Keep a tight grip on what you were taught, whether in personal conversation or by our letter. May Jesus himself and God our Father, who reached out in love and surprised you with gifts of unending help and confidence, put a fresh heart in you, invigorate your work, enliven your speech.

—2 Thessalonians. 2:15-17

# PUTTIN' ON AND PEEKIN' IN

*B*E CAREFUL WHAT you pray for! A few years before my breast cancer experience, I had asked God to make me more real. You see, I am not a natural beauty and I never have been. The thought of going out of my house without makeup puts chills down my spine. My skin is splotchy, my eyes fade into my head, and post-chemo, I have very few eyebrows. Estee Lauder is high up there on my list of favorite women. What God hasn't given me naturally, I put on. It is just astonishing what a little foundation, mascara, brow pencil, and lipstick will do!

But what is true in my physical life is even more essential in my spiritual walk. I am lacking many things in my soul, but if I allow Him, my Lord helps me put on His beauty, and He is the ultimate makeup artist. Some days, I forget to ask Him to put His beauty in me. But on the days when I remember, He does amazing things! Now these things are not necessarily life-changing, but they are certainly life-enhancing, for the moment at least. They put a smile on a face and lift up a discouraged heart, and suddenly, by the grace of God living in each one of us, someone feels loved.

I experienced a sweet situation like that on a visit to see my mother, who has dementia. I was to fly back home that afternoon, so I wanted to spend that morning talking to her and ministering to her. But she spent the entire morning dozing on and off, even as I curled and brushed her hair and creamed her hands and feet. I finally just read my Bible, the whole time whining to God about my lack of time spent with her. Then it happened.

God gave me His eyes to see the other ladies in the room and His heart for them, too. They, too, needed ministry and a loving touch. So I asked each of them if I could polish their fingernails, and they were so excited. The ninety-eight-year old lady, who had an enormous black eye from falling two days prior, did not speak, but as I made her nails look pretty, her little eyes just sparkled and her smile spoke loudly of the joy in her heart from being acknowledged and affirmed.

The other lady, who was very vocal, couldn't believe that I would polish her nails for free. But after I did, she waved to me every time our paths crossed. I had said, "I will minister to my mother today," but God had said, "Let Me minister to these other ladies through you."

The next time I flew to see my mom, I asked about the dear little lady with the bright eyes, and she had died. I said a grateful prayer to my compassionate Savior for not letting me miss that moment to bless her. Symbolically, I had put beautiful shoes on her that day, thanks to God's intervention, and I don't know which one of us was more thrilled about it.

A verse in Philippians has always made me tremble and it speaks to this mind-set that Christ wants us to have. "But I press on, that I may lay hold of that for which Christ Jesus has also laid hold of me" (Phil. 3:12 NKJV).

If I understand this verse correctly, it says that Jesus Christ, Who died for me, has specific purposes for which He laid hold of me. Having breast cancer does not nullify that verse. He can still use each one of us to touch the lives of other people in His divine design. Maybe just having a cheerful attitude while receiving chemotherapy or a confident trust that is apparent to the X-ray technician or even something as small as a smile or a tender hug for a sister who is feeling down. It's all about helping others as we all walk this breast cancer journey together.

When I get to heaven, I know I won't have tears over my sins because Jesus paid for them all; but I pray that I will not have tears for people whom Jesus wanted me to touch with His love, but I did not. If any lives were left a little more discouraged or despairing because of words I did not say—how tragic, how needless. Submission to His work in our lives, no matter how broken our lives are at the time, brings blessings for everyone. So even as you walk your rocky road, ask God to give you His eyes and His heart for others. "Put on" His heart, and then "peek in" to their lives with the love of Christ.

"My dear children, let's not just talk about love; let's practice real love. This is the only way we'll know we're living truly, living in God's reality" (1 John 3:18-19).

> My beloved friends, let us continue to love each other since love comes from God. Everyone who loves is born of God and experiences a relationship with God. The person who refuses to love doesn't know the first thing about God, because God *is* love—so you can't know him if you don't love. This is how God showed his love for us: God sent his only Son into the world so we might live through him. This is the kind of love we are talking about—not that we once upon a time loved God, but that he loved us and sent his Son as a sacrifice to clear away our sins and the damage they've done to our relationship with God. My dear, dear friends, if God loved us like this, we certainly ought to love each other. No one has seen God, ever. But if we love one another, God dwells deeply within us, and his love becomes complete in us—perfect love!
>
> —1 John 4:7-12

> All praise to the God and Father of our Master, Jesus the Messiah! Father of all mercy! God of all healing counsel! He comes alongside us when we go through hard times, and before you know it, he brings us alongside someone else who is going through hard times so that we can be there for that person just as God was there for us. We have plenty of hard times that come from following the Messiah, but no more so than the good times of his healing comfort—we get a full measure of that, too.
>
> —2 Corinthians 1:3-5

# SCATTER JOY!

*I*T IS A pretty pink-and-green-striped wooden frame, holding a picture of my husband, ministering to a Haitian child, and the inscription says, "Scatter Joy!" It is the heart of the gospel. Peter said it to the lame man in Acts 3:6, "Silver and gold I do not have, but what I do have I give to you: In the name of Jesus Christ of Nazareth, rise up and walk" (NKJV).

What I have I give to you. So what do you have that you can give to others? Jesus made that very plain one day after healing a demon-possessed man. The now-lucid man asked to go with Jesus, but His response was, "'Go home to your own people. Tell them your story—what the Master did, how he had mercy on you.' The man went back and began to preach in the Ten Towns area about what Jesus had done for him. He was the talk of the town" (Mark 5:18-20).

What Jesus said to him, He says to each of us: Tell your story. Scatter the joy that knowing Jesus brings—what He has done for you and how He has had mercy on you. Yes, there have been difficult, uphill roads—paths so steep you thought you'd never catch your breath, but the Lord guided you through those hard times and brought blessings in the midst of the pain. Someone desperately needs to hear that story. What makes this such a wonderful assignment from the Lord is that it is foolproof. It is easy to talk about because you've lived it, and no one can dispute it because there is no denying that it happened to you. There have been frightening times, when the Lord calmed your fears;

exhausting times, when the hand of God raised you up again. There have been moments when the outpouring of His love, through others, has made you cry and places that were once broken that now are whole, and your joy can't be contained. You need to scatter it—let it multiply as it refreshes others, too. It is about giving away what you have, which no one can ever take from you.

I began this book with my life verse, 1 Peter 3:15, which says to "always be ready to give a defense to everyone who asks you a reason for the hope that is in you" (NKJV). Pray daily for God to bring people across your path to whom you can tell your story. Sometimes it will just be a few words of encouragement to give them the shoes they need for that day's path. Other times, you might have a chance to tell more of your story. Just ask God to show you whom to touch with Jesus' love. In your interactions with others, gracefully tell them a little bit of what Jesus has done for you. It's as easy as that. If you've never really thought about what your story is, then spend some quiet time thinking about how Jesus has touched you and healed you, redeemed you and delivered you. God can use these little scatterings of joy or tiny bits of your story in ways you could never imagine. Those daily "Yeses" of obedience to Him can mean a great deal in another's pink journey.

In God's hands, our little offerings can be supernaturally multiplied for His purposes and His glory. So scatter joy wherever you go. Tell the story of how Jesus has touched you, even on this difficult path, and how He has shown you mercy. Have beautiful feet for Jesus, like it says in Isaiah 52:7: "How beautiful on the mountains are the feet of the messenger bringing good news, breaking the news that all's well, proclaiming good times, announcing salvation, telling (insert a sister's name), 'Your God reigns!'"

"What matters most to me is to finish what God started: the job the Master Jesus gave me of letting everyone I meet know all about this incredibly extravagant generosity of God" (Acts 20:24).

"But how can people call for help if they don't know who to trust? And how can they know who to trust if they haven't heard of the One who can be trusted? And how can they hear if nobody tells them?" (Rom. 10:14).

Here's another way to put it: You're here to be light, bringing out the God-colors in the world. God is not a secret to be kept. We're going public with this, as public as a city on a hill. If I make you light-bearers, you don't think I'm going to hide you under a bucket, do you? I'm putting you on a light stand. Now that I've put you there on a hilltop, on a light stand—shine! Keep open house; be generous with your lives. By opening up to others, you'll prompt people to open up with God, this generous Father in heaven.

—Matthew 5:14-16

"We saw it, we heard it, and now we're telling you so you can experience it along with us, this experience of communion with the Father and his Son, Jesus Christ. Our motive for writing is simply this: We want you to enjoy this, too. Your joy will double our joy!" (1 John 1:3-4).

"Now to Him who is able to keep you from stumbling, and to present you faultless before the presence of His glory with exceeding joy, to God our Savior, Who alone is wise, be glory and majesty, dominion and power, both now and forever. Amen" (Jude 24 NKJV).

# WALK IN FAITH

*T*HE DESIGN OF the shirt was so "me." It was a hot pink shirt with lime green lettering, and it said, "Walk in Faith," but the "t" in *faith* was a big cross. My dear friends, who designed this shirt and organized the walk on my behalf, knew me well. They fashioned the shirt to reflect my personality and tastes, and they missed not one detail.

In a more profound and perfect way, our sovereign Lord designs each of our individual breast cancer walks with His perfect knowledge of not only who we are, but also who He plans for us to become. Because He is not bound by time or space, He can be with us as we walk our journey and also go ahead of us to prepare the way for us.

There is a wonderful analogy for our breast cancer journey in the Gospels, and I want to share it with you as an encouragement for your walk. Here are three passages that represent the three different stages of Jesus' road to Jerusalem and to the cross. Jerusalem meant suffering, sacrifice, and separation to Jesus. We all have Jerusalems in our lives—those places in our journeys where we're sure there is going to be sacrifice, separation, or suffering. Our breast cancer journey is a perfect example. The first of those scriptures, Mark 10:32, depicts Jesus as He *anticipates* the cross. "Back on the road, they set out for Jerusalem. Jesus had a head start on them, and they were following, puzzled and not just a little afraid." The next verse, Luke 23:26, shows the *actuality* of the cross: "As they led him off, they made Simon, a man from Cyrene who happened to be coming in from the countryside, carry the cross behind Jesus." The last verse, Mark 16:6-7, corresponds to the *aftermath* of the cross. (This is the angel speaking to the women at the tomb of Jesus). He said, "Don't be afraid. I know you are looking for Jesus the Nazarene, the One they nailed on the cross. He's been raised up; he's here no longer. You can see for yourselves that the place is empty. Now—on your way. Tell his disciples and Peter that he is going on ahead of you to Galilee. You'll see him there, exactly as he said."

Did you catch it? In every step of Jesus' terrible journey, whether it was the anticipation, the actuality or the aftermath, He was always *ahead* of the disciples. I believe that God was very deliberate in pointing that out to us, and do you know why? There are places, just like the disciples, where we are "puzzled and not just a little afraid." But God longs for us to really know, not only in our minds, but also in our hearts, that Jesus is walking ahead of us on that puzzling, frightening journey, preparing the path for us in the way that He knows is the best. So whether we are just anticipating the realities of this breast cancer path, are in the actual throes of it, or are in its aftermath, Jesus is not only with us, but He is ahead of us, preparing the next step for us.

My friend Elizabeth had a situation in her family that relates perfectly to this lesson. Her husband took their two girls on a camping trip every year, but Elizabeth had never gone. She wasn't overwhelmed at the thought of going on a camping trip, and it was just easier for her to stay home with their young son. But this particular year she knew she had no valid excuses left and she needed to go. After the weekend, she related a moment of that adventure which really resounded in my heart. Her oldest daughter, Sarah, was so excited to take her to a special place she knew about from her previous trips. When they got there, she said to her mom, "See, *this* is what I wanted to show you!"

I was so touched by the spiritual lesson in that story that I journalled these thoughts, "Lord, forgive me for doubting You when You take me places where I have been afraid to go—places I've never been before! Make me more willing to go to those places with You, Lord, and see the things You want to show me."

My friend, Van, pegged cancer perfectly (she knew from hard experience with both parents). She said, "Cancer just speeds up life.

You have all the natural highs and lows; they are just condensed into a smaller time frame." How true that is. None of us need reminders of our path to Jerusalem right now; that fact is all too clear. What we need every day is time to put those facts aside and focus on the Truth, the Lord of our paths.

This is an arduous journey, and the strength and grace needed to walk it in a manner worthy of the Lord only come through time spent with Him. So wherever you are on that journey to Jerusalem, spend as much time as you can with the Lord, Who blazed that path. Read and reread whatever devotion meets your need at that particular moment, but stay close to Him. For only God can give you the shoes you need for this difficult path. But you can be sure that the shoes He will give you will be victorious, I-win-in-the-end, to-God-be-the-glory shoes. So walk your journey in faith because He is leading you. Thanks be to God!

Do you see what this means—all these pioneers who blazed the way, all these veterans cheering us on? It means we'd better get on with it. Strip down, start running—and never quit! So don't sit around on your hands! No more dragging your feet! Clear the path for long-distance runners so no one will trip and fall, so no one will step in a hole and sprain an ankle. Help each other out. And run for it!
—Hebrews 12:1, 12-13

May God, who puts all things together, makes all things whole, who made a lasting mark through the sacrifice of Jesus, the sacrifice of blood that sealed the eternal covenant, who led Jesus, our Great Shepherd, up and alive from the dead, now put you together, provide you with everything you need to please him, make us into what gives him most pleasure, by means of the sacrifice of Jesus, the Messiah. All glory to Jesus forever and always! Oh yes, yes, yes.
—Hebrews 13:20-21

# ENDNOTES

1. Eugene H. Peterson, *A Long Obedience in the Same Direction* (Downers Grove, Illinois: InterVarsity Press, 2000), 191.
2. Charles Haddon Spurgeon, *Strengthen My Spirit* (Uhrichsville, Ohio: Barbour Publishing, 2004), August 30.
3. A. W. Tozer, *We Travel an Appointed Way*, quoted in Robert J. Morgan's *The Red Sea Rules* (Nashville, Tennessee: Thomas Nelson, 2001), 12.
4. Charles Haddon Spurgeon, quoted in Ruth and Warren Myers' *31 Days of Praise* (Sisters, Oregon: Multnomah Publishers, 1994), 19.

# INDEX

For more information or to contact Linda Grabeman,
please visit her Web site, NoPrissyShoes.com, or
e-mail her at Linda@NoPrissyShoes.com.

CPSIA information can be obtained at www.ICGtesting.com
Printed in the USA
LVOW060530120712

289656LV00001B/6/P